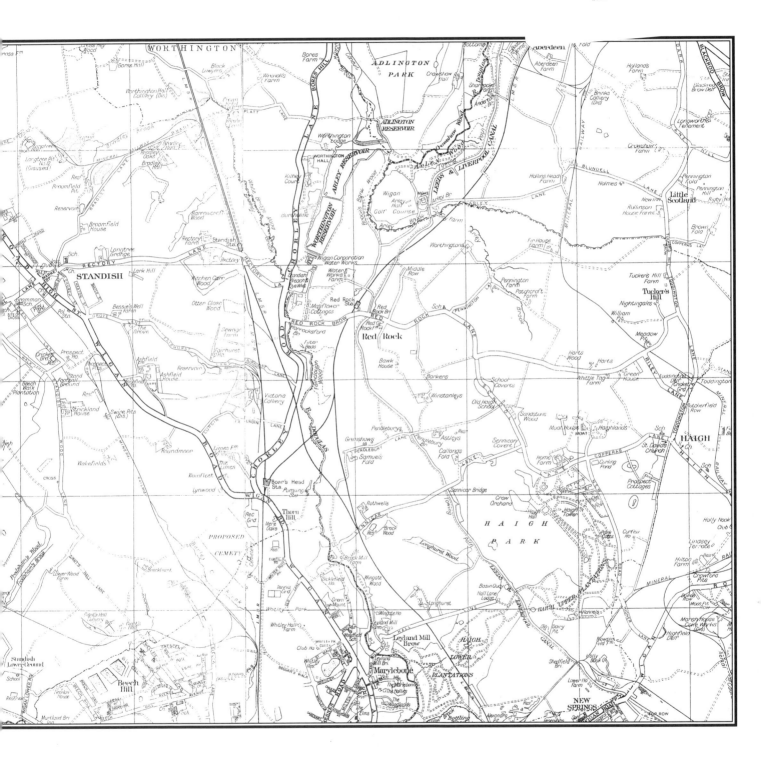

ACKNOWLEDGEMENTS

My first duty is to record sincere thanks to all those people who have in any way whatsoever contributed to make the completion of this book possible. There are a number who have specifically requested that their names should not appear on a formal acknowledgement list. Whilst I respect their wishes, I am nevertheless equally indebted to them for their kindness.

Alan and Enid Andrews	Edingburgh Drive, Pemberton, Wigan
Nora Arnold	Wigan Road, Standish
Alice Birchall	Primrose Lane, Standish
Joan Birchall	Foxholes, Horwich
Frank and Betty Calderbank	Wrightington
Ted Cheetham	Inward Drive, Shevington
Robert Coote	Sandy Lane, Hindley
Maureen Critchley	Highfield Drive, Standish
Gerrard Thomas	Shevington
Reverend Michael Everitt	St. Wilfrid's Parish Church, Standish
Ronnie Hunt	Wigan
Ron Kaye	Thirlmere Avenue, Standish
Josie Makinson	Preston Road, Standish
Father S. Maloney	St.Marie's Church, Standish
Marjorie Mason	Church Road, Astley, Tyldesley
Monica Reid	Bentham Road, Standish
Colin de Rouffignac	Appley Bridge
Betty Simm, (nee Cowburn)	Bentham Road, Standish
Brian Winrow	Scot Lane, Aspull

Books by the same author:

About Horwich	ISBN No. 0 950877271*
Rivington, Lancashire	ISBN No. 0 95087728X*
Adlington & District, Lancashire	ISBN No. 0 1873500017*
About Blackrod	ISBN No. 1 873500025
Old Rivington & DIstrict	ISBN No. 0 952618710
Horwich Locomotive Works	ISBN No. 0 952618729
A Short History of Heath Charnock Isolation Hospital	
Leverhulme's Rivington	ISBN No. 0 952618737
More About Horwich	ISBN No. 0 952618745
About Haigh & Aspull	ISBN No. 0 952618753
About Anglezarke	ISBN No. 0 952618761

*Currently out of print

Front cover - water colour painting of Market Place, Standish, about 1900,
by Jill M. Aldersley of Ambleside, Cumbria.
Front end papers - Map of the Standish area

ABOUT STANDISH
by
M. D. Smith

This book is dedicated to the memory of Fred Arnold
on behalf of his wife, Nora, and his two sons, John and Michael.

Fred Arnold
1928 - 1995

Wyre Publishing
c/o David Smith, 27 Sutton Lane, Adlington, Lancashire PR6 9PA

TABLE OF CONTENTS

EDMUND (TED) CHEETHAM.

*Ted Cheetham of Inward Drive, Shevington, assisted
greatly in the compilation of this work. Sadly, he died
before seeing the book in print and this dedication to him
is made on behalf of his wife and family.*

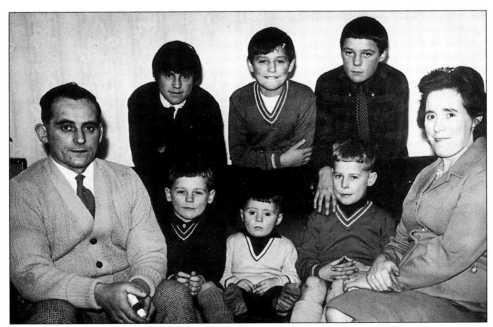

Ted and Martha Cheetham with their children, 1967

INTRODUCTION

Originally, it was my intention to write a history of Standish, which would include references to Adlington, Anderton, Heath Charnock, Duxbury and Coppull. I have previously written a history of the Adlington district, which was published in 1988, but the book has long been out of print. It therefore seemed an ideal opportunity to combine new material with what was, in effect, a re-issue of the earlier book.

Having read the History of Standish, written by Thomas Cruddas Porteus, I soon became aware that the project was far too large and unwieldy. Reverend Porteus reached a similar conclusion and seems to have resolved it in much the same way that I have, by confining the book to Standish with only brief references to the out townships.

Standish comprises ten townships, eleven if Standish and Langtree are treated separately. The remaining ones, not mentioned in the first paragraph, are Charnock Richard, Shevington, Welch Whittle and Worthington.

It has been an extremely interesting exercise to compile the material and illustrations for this book. I have received a great deal of assistance from many sources, particularly the local inhabitants. The greater credit for this work belongs to them.

There are a number of excellent publications already in existence covering various aspects of the history of Standish. I sincerely hope that the contents of this book augment those earlier works and create an awareness of the richness of our heritage.

Malcolm David Smith
27 Sutton Lane
Adlington
Lancashire
PR6 9PA
April 2003.

First published 2003
Copyright © 2003 M. D. Smith
ISBN

Graphic layout by Highlight Type Bureau Ltd, Bradford
Printed by The Amadeus Press, Cleckheaton

Market Street, Standish, circa 1920.

This interesting old photograph shows the entrance to Standish, with High Street on the left and the junction of Church Street to the right, circa 1900. Visible in the centre is the frontage of what is now the Globe Inn but which, at that time, was two separate public houses, standing back to back, the Globe Inn and the White Lion Inn. In the centre is Queen Victoria's Jubilee Fountain. The Standish War Memorial was erected behind the fountain, on the 17th April 1920, following the First World War.

ABOUT
STANDISH

Brief history of the Manor of Standish

The name, Standish, is derived from the Old English 'stan-edisc' meaning 'stony pasture'. The history of Standish, prior to the Norman Conquest of 1066, is obscure but Standish is thought to have been one of the twelve considerable towns in the south of Lancashire in which the Saxons erected fortified castles for the residence of their chiefs and the protection of the country.

Nearby Blackrod was once thought to be the Roman Station known as Coccium, which existed at the time of Antoninus. Some historians have identified Standish as Coccium, although it is now generally accepted that Wigan has the strongest claim.

There have been two important discoveries of Roman coins in the Standish district. Doctor Charles Leigh, great-grandson of the Rector of Standish, recorded the first of these finds in 1700. A ploughman working at or near Standish unearthed a copper vessel known as either an urceolus or a patella. This contained 200 silver denarii dating from 90 A.D. to 240 A.D., along with two massive gold rings and an intaglio or signet for setting in a ring. The signet bore an engraving, thought to be a figure of the Roman God 'Mars'. Sadly, the whereabouts of this find are not known.

The second hoard of Roman coins was found on the 20th January 1926, on Bolton Field, Standish, which lies behind the villa 'Minerva' on the east side of Wigan Lane, a few yards from the Wigan boundary. This property was, at the time, under construction. A labourer digging a shallow trench came across several coins fused together in twos and threes, which had obviously been in a container of which no trace was remaining. In total, 140 silver denarii were found ranging in date from the time of the Emperor Nero, to the reign of Alexander Severus. One of the coins was taken to Mr. A.J.Hawkes, the Wigan Borough Librarian, who, realising the significance of the find, not only succeeded in getting all the coins identified by an expert but also managed to secure them for preservation in the public library.

Prior to the Norman Conquest of 1066, the lands between the River Ribble and the River Mersey belonged to the Crown. Following the Norman Invasion, William the Conqueror was crowned King William 1, at Westminster Abbey on Christmas Day 1066.

The newly crowned King rewarded his allies with the grant of lands. Roger de Poitou, who was the son of the King's cousin, Roger of Montgomery, received the lands referred to above along with estates in various parts of England, collectively known as the 'honour of Lancaster'.

A few years after being awarded these lands in 1068, Roger de Poitou was banished from the Kingdom for conspiring with Robert, the eldest son of William 1, to overthrow the King. The Crown re-possessed his estates.

High Street, Standish, circa 1920.

Warin de Bussel took part in the Norman Invasion of 1066 and is believed to have been chief adviser to Roger of Montgomery. He married Roger's niece, Amiera, and was granted various lands. His son eventually became Baron of Penwortham, which lies in the Leyland Hundred and includes both Standish and Langtree.

Richard de Bussel, who was grandson of the above named, Warin de Bussel, gave two carucates of land in Standish and Langtree, to Richard Spileman, on the latter's marriage to his sister in 1153. A carucate was an amount of land such as one team of oxen could plough in a season.

The family, de Bussel, were in fact the progenitors of the Standish line but precise details of the descent are unclear. It appears, however, that Richard Spileman's only daughter married a man named Leising, who is believed to have been one of the first rectors of Standish Church. The couple had two sons, Radulphus and Siward, who inherited the manors of Standish and Langtree. Eventually, in 1206, the brothers separated the townships and divided the advowson for Standish Church. In common with accepted practice, Radulphus adopted the name 'de Standish' from that of his manorial seat, and Siward became 'de Langtree' after the name of his manor.

Church advowsons included the right to appoint a lay rector, who did not officiate at services but appointed a priest whom he supported. The main part of his duty was to take charge of church lands and administer them by arrangement with the lord of the manor. Any rents or tithes obtained were shared with the manorial lord. All family matters, legal disputes, weddings and funerals, were taken care of by the rector, who naturally protected the welfare and interests of the family who appointed him. An advowson was therefore a powerful and lucrative privilege.

On his marriage to Juliana, Radulphus de Standish began acquiring lands and by 1240 the family owned both Standish and Langtree manors along with the full advowson for Standish Church. The Standish family coat of arms consists of three upright, cupped dishes or tun dishes. This armorial bearing was in use by the family until the sixteenth century when it was replaced by an owl with a rat in its talons.

There is a wealth of published material concerning the noble Standish family. Much of it stems from the transcription of legal documents, dating back to the thirteenth century, which were donated to Wigan Library on the death of the last surviving family member.

Thomas Cruddas Porteus, M.A., B.D., Vicar of St. John the Divine, Coppull, relied heavily on these papers for the detail in his book, 'The History of Standish', which was funded by public subscription and published in 1927. Reverend Porteus was a thorough and meticulous researcher whose work remains a lasting testament to his extraordinary talent.

Ownership of the lands within Standish parish changed frequently down the centuries and whilst it is not intended to provide an exact chronological record of the various holders, references will be made, as appropriate, to the individual owners and events affecting the district.

ARMORIAL BEARINGS OF LOCAL FAMILIES

STANDISH OF STANDISH

STANDISH (Ancient):
Argent, a saltire, within a bordure
engrailed, *sable*.

ARMS BORNE BY JOHN DE STANDISH,
1332: *Argent*, a saltire between
four crosses patonce, *sable*.

ARMS: *Azure*, three standing dishes, *argent*.
CREST: A cock, *sable*, beaked, wattled, combed, legged,
and spurred, *or*.

LANGTREE OF LANGTREE

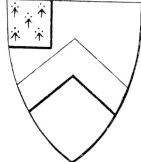

ARMS: *Sable*, a chevron, *argent*, a
canton, *ermine*.
CREST: A sacre or saker with wings
expanded, *gules*, membered, *or*.

STANDISH OF DUXBURY

ARMS: *Sable*, three standing dishes, *argent*.
CREST: An owl with a rat in its talons, proper.

*Example of a silver and enamel medallion awarded to
past Chairmen of the Urban District of Standish-with-
Langtree.*

10

Thomas Cruddas Porteus, author of the 'History of Standish', was Vicar of the church of St. John the Divine Church, Coppull, between 1912 and 1934.

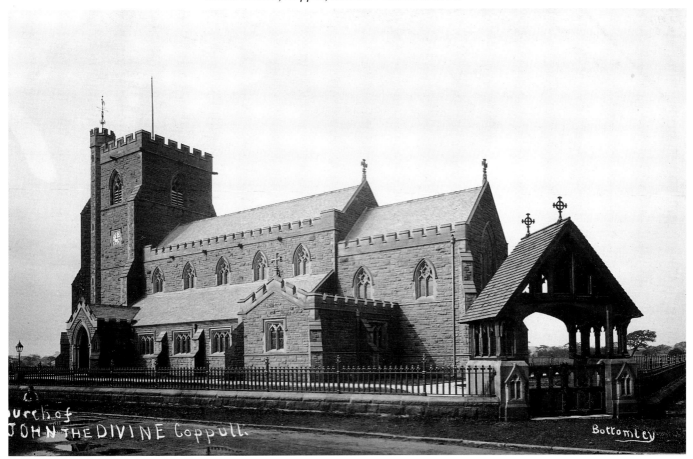

An exterior view of the church of St. John the Divine, Coppull, dated circa 1920.

Reproduced below are copies of correspondence between Thomas Cruddas Porteus and T. Meadows, Esq., of the Wigan Observer newspaper.

T. Meadows, Esq.

The "Observer" Office,

Wallgate,

Wigan.

St. John's Vicarage,
Coppull,
Chorley.
28 Sep. '27.

Dear Mr Meadows,

I forgot to mention that Wigan Library has been supplied with copies of my book. There is just a chance that some journalist might see them, so I have sent a note to Mr. Hawkes asking him to hold them back if possible.

Yours faithfully
T. C. Porteus

P.S. The Preston Guardian (Toolmin) & also wants subscribers; but I am holding this copy back for a time.

12

ST. JOHN'S VICARAGE,
COPPULL,
CHORLEY,
LANCASHIRE.
13 - XI - 29

REV. T. C. PORTEUS.

Dear Mr Meadows,

Many thanks for the excellent notice you gave of my book in last weeks Wigan Observer and my reference to Standish. I am made to Standish landmark to so some statement — refuted upon that seem the Standish family that the Standish would object to the Reformed Church.

Many you would hardly keep the statement became a new. There is Church Reformation Standish at — the Reformation they on friendly evidence entered on the Rectors, and family entered with the Rectors, and terms with the Rectors, the right although deprived, they became is nominate Rectors. The right the laws by leaving who to nominate. I show this the nomination. I show this could appointed in my history of Chorley in my history of ...

Standish (p. 82). Charles Standish was the patron as late as 1877 and sold the advowson then.

I am very unlikely then, that the Standishes without their built property title the Church. By the way to the Church always had a spire, from the 14th century at least. Activated by the commercial spirit of people temporarily allowed a beautiful buildings to be endow and hidden. "So the Rev's (so called) was a market place site and the upper stories appear to have been used for storing grain and cattle food to sell to small holders and others who came to market.

A similar position has arisen at Wigan, where lofty building (partially) hide the old Church.

The public spirit of Mr J. M. Ainscough, the donor of the property, is a splendid example of rural patriotism.

Yours sincerely,
T. C. Porteus

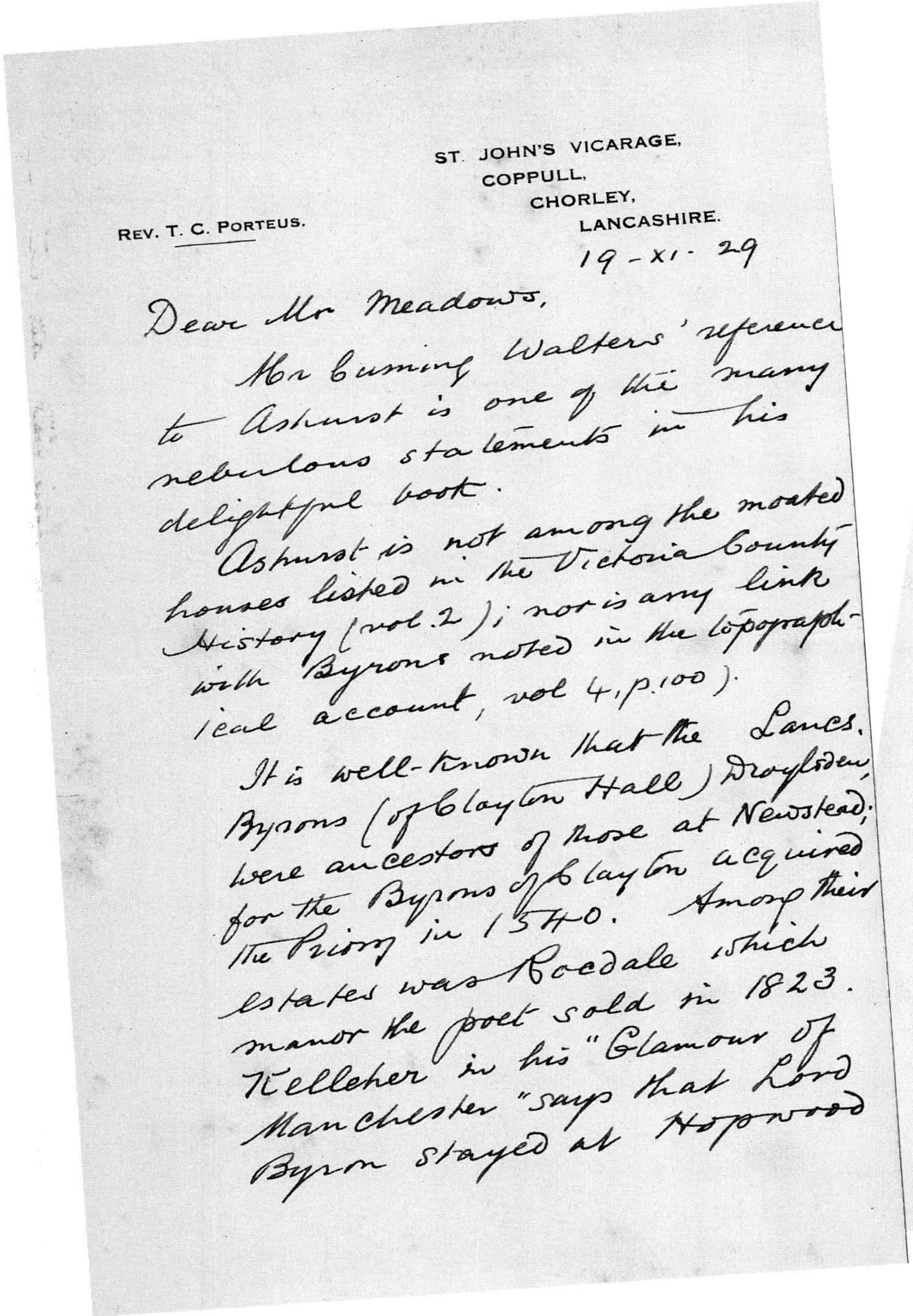

ST. JOHN'S VICARAGE,
COPPULL,
CHORLEY,
LANCASHIRE.

19 - XI - 29

REV. T. C. PORTEUS.

Dear Mr Meadows,

For buying Walters' reference
Ashurst is one of his many
to Ashurst sto tenements in his
nebulous book.

delightful book.

Ashurst is not among the moated
houses listed in the Victoria County
History (vol 2); nor is any link
with Byrons noted in the topographical account, vol 4 p.210). Lancs.

It is well-known that the
Byrons (of Clayton Hall) Droylsden,
were ancestors of hope at Newstead,
were ancestors of Clayton acquired
for the Byrons in 1540. Among their
estates was Rochdale which
the poet sold in 1823.

Wellesley in his "Glamour of
Manchester" says that Lord
Byron stayed at Hopwood

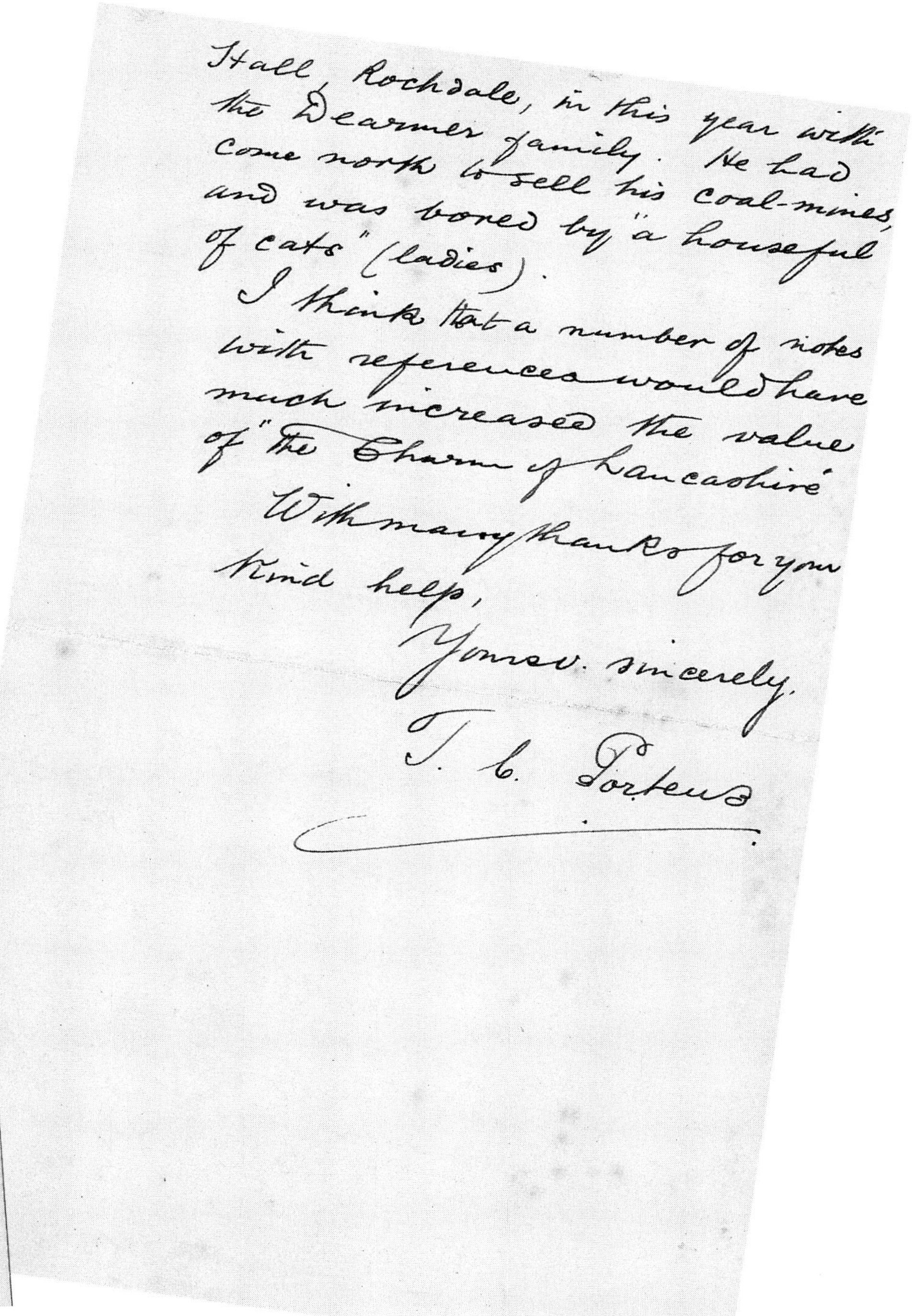

Hall Rochdale, in this year with
the Dearmer family. He had
come north to sell his coal-mines
and was stoned by a houseful
of cats" (ladies).

I think that a number of notes
with references would there
mean increased the value
of the Charm of Lancashire.

With many thanks for your
kind help,

Yours sincerely,

T. C. Porteus

ST. JOHN'S VICARAGE.
COPPULL.
CHORLEY.
LANCASHIRE.
2 - ii - '31

REV. T. C. PORTEUS.

Dear Mr Meadows,

for best in the W.O. you give a view

Saturday, Sept 11, 1859. Church before 1859, of Standish. There were 3 galleries, stating that there were in fact only two. at the — there were in fact only two, in my History drawing facing p. 60 that there of Standish makes it clear that the South side, there was no gallery on the South side. It was at — was a faculty in 1825 a faculty was ob- although in 1825 a faculty was ob- tained for placing one there. See p. 60.

p. the woodwork as it resembles a pillory, as it now resembles a pillory with on the South side, to the old pulpit is now on or in your view. The pulpit with in your view. The pulpit is now facing (P. 80) stair rail. See was facing South, the north side, see was facing South, but was before 1859 on the — opposite page but was before 1859 mentioned opposite page as the other view mentioned 60 makes evident.

Some weeks ago you asked a question in the W.O. re yew trees at Standish. I was then unable to reply through ill-health. It is in the W.O. — rectory. I was then unable to reply through ill-health. It is interesting to note that in the

Year 1810 under date 20th May Rev Richard Perryn, Rector of Standish, made the following entry in his "Notitia" or Diary:

"Measured the girth of the yew trees upon the hillock in the Rector's garden, when the East tree, at a yard from the ground appeared to be 8 feet 5 inches, and the West tree at the same height 6 feet 5 inches. When these trees were planted there is no memorial."

If you print a note about these matters, please do not mention my name as contributing information. For I am retiring from parochial work at present.

With kind regards,
Yours sincerely,
T. C. Porteus.

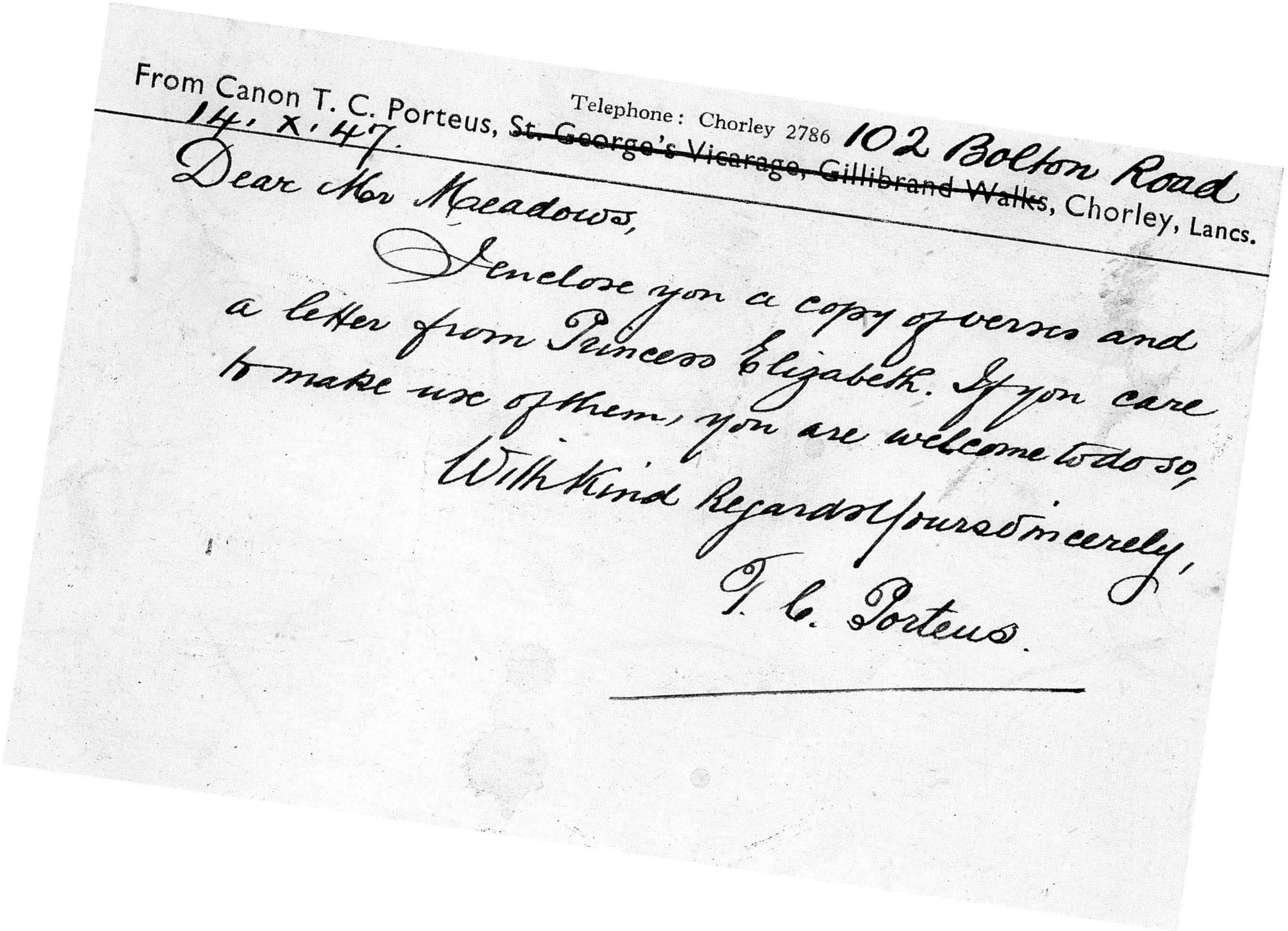

From Canon T.C. Porteus, St. George's Vicarage, Gillibrand Walks, Chorley, Lancs.

Telephone: Chorley 2786

102 Bolton Road

14. X. 47.

Dear Mrs Meadows,

I enclose you a copy of verses and a letter from Frances Elizabeth. If you care to make use of them, you are welcome to do so.

With kind regards,

Yours sincerely,

T. C. Porteus.

In the reign of Edward 11 (1307-1327) the principal townships in the parish of Standish were held as follows. Adam Banastre held Shevington; Jordan de Standish held Standish; H.de Langtree held Langtree, Hugh de Adlington and Adam de Duxbery held moieties of Adlington and Duxbury; Thomas Banastre held one-third and Hugh Gogard two-thirds of Heath Charnock; H.de Chernock held one-half of Charnock Richard, and H.de Lea the other half, and Welsh (Welch) Whittle was held by a person whose surname is lost. Sir Adam de Banastre subsequently forfeited most of his estate due to his involvement in the Banastre Rebellion of 1315 against the Earl of Lancaster and his baronial party. Hugh de Standish supported the Earl of Lancaster and received most of the lands forfeited. However, the Duxbury family managed to retain a sizeable estate, which their descendants eventually sold to Ralph Standish, lord of Standish Manor, in the sixteenth century.

In 1340, the Hundred Years War commenced between England and France. Hostilities opened with the total destruction of the French fleet off Sluys. At the Battle of Crecy, in 1346, the English king, Edward 111, achieved victory over the French forces. The King's son, Prince Edward (the Black Prince) was knighted on the battlefield. Ralph de Standish was probably involved in this battle then being of similar age to Prince Edward, that is 16 years old.

Richard 11 came to the English throne in 1377 when only ten years of age. Four years later, in 1381, he was left to deal with the 'Peasants' Revolt'. Grievances of the peasants centred on unfair taxes, a similar situation to the Poll Tax experienced in recent years. Their elected leader and spokesman was Wat Tyler. The protestors marched to the capital in order to bring their cause to the notice of the King. Surprisingly, they virtually captured London and even accepted the surrender of the Tower of London. Several exchanges took place between the King and Wat Tyler. At the last of these, on Saturday 15th June 1381, Wat Tyler is reported to have drawn his dagger in the presence of the monarch. In the confusion that followed, Ralph de Standish ran Tyler through with his sword, killing him. Soon after the revolt was put down, Ralph de Standish received a knighthood for services in defence of the King at Smithfield. He was afterwards known as the King's Knight.

In 1388-9 Robert de Standish was appointed as sheriff of Lancashire. The position required that he entered into a recognisance in the sum of £200 to account to the King and John of Gaunt for his execution of his public duty. Three years later, Rafe Standish of Standish was appointed to the same office.

At the Battle of Agincourt, fought on the 25th October 1415, Sir Rowland de Standish, James de Standish and John de Chisnal, each with six footmen behind him, were amongst the army of Henry V. The English force was outnumbered by the French three to one but managed a stunning victory in which 6,000 Frenchmen were slain with the loss of fewer than 400 English troops. It was Sir Rowland de Standish who brought home the relics of St. Laurence from Normandy to Chorley.

Sir Ralph Standish, a kinsman of the King's Knight, was killed at Gerberoy in France during 1434 whilst commanding soldiers in a battle against the French.

For heroism at the Battle of Hutton Field in Scotland, during 1482, Sir Alexander Standish was made a knight-banneret (a higher class of knight, inferior to a Baron).

Constance Gerard, an eighth generation descendant of King William the Lion of Scotland, married Alexander Standish, later lord of Standish manor, in the fifteenth century.

During the Wars of the Roses, a series of civil wars in England during the reigns of Henry V1 (1422-1471), Edward 1V (1461-1483) and Richard 111 (1483-1485); the influence of the Stanley family in the Standish district was strengthened. The Harrington family owned lands in Standish, Heath Charnock and Shevington, which were accounted parcels of the manor and Castle of Hornby. Sir Thomas Harrington of Hornby took the side of the Yorkists and along with his son, Sir John Harrington, was killed in the Battle of Wakefield fought in 1460. Another son, Sir James Harrington, lost the manor of Hornby and its appurtenances, by forfeiture, in 1486; and these lands came to Sir Edward Stanley, son of the first Earl of Derby, by grant of the King.

One of the staunchest critics of the religious revolution in the sixteenth century, which had its beginnings between the years 1533 to 1539, and was known as the 'Reformation', was John Standish. He was a native of Standish and had been educated at Brasenose College, Oxford, afterwards becoming a Fellow of Whittington College, London. He died in 1556, Canon at Worcester. Locally, there was much resistance to the new religious order particularly from the most zealous Roman Catholic families who included the Standishes of Standish Hall, the Houghtons of Park Hall in Charnock Richard, the Rigbys of Burgh in Duxbury, and the Worthingtons of Blainscough in Coppull.

There were many recusants (one who refuses to acknowledge the supremacy of the sovereign in religious matters) in the district, some of whom suffered persecution for their beliefs.

Edward Standish held the Manor of Standish for 59 years from 1551 until 1610. Edward and his brother Ralph were only six and nine years old respectively on the death of their father, Alexander, in 1539. In view of their age, the manor was claimed by the Crown and granted to the Earl of Derby. The two brothers were given into the custody of their grandmother, Alice. Ralph died in 1547, and Edward succeeded to Standish Manor on reaching the age of 18 in 1551. Edward married twice, being the first Standish lord to do so. His first wife was Ellen Radcliffe, the daughter of Sir William Radcliffe of Ordsall, Manchester. Following her death, he married Elizabeth Towneley of Towneley Manor. Edward Standish had six sons and two daughters by marriage.

Standish Hall was built in 1574 as the new manor house for the estate. The building was of Tudor design and of the favoured H construction. It consisted of oak timbers and plaster on a brick base. There was a large courtyard and stabling at the rear. The property was surrounded by a moat.

Standish Hall, Standish, circa 1920.
The hall was built in 1574 and was the manorial seat of the Standish family.

Park Hall, Charnock Richard, circa 1900.

Etching of St. Wilfrid's Parish Church, Standish, circa 1880.

A monument to Captain Myles Standish erected in Duxbury, Massachusetts, United States of America.

The legend reads, "In memory of CAPTAIN MYLES STANDISH, the only trained soldier in the Pilgrim community, always their military commander but also a valuable civil servant and a wise promoter of the business interests of the Pilgrim Stock Company. In fight fearless, impetuous and resolute, in civil affairs, cautious and firm, in business, shrewd, just and far seeing. A conscientious and high-minded leader of devout men and women who founded in a wilderness a tolerant church and a free state".

Captain Myles Standish's grave which is situated in Duxbury, Massachusetts, U.S.A.

*Replica of Captain Myles Standish's ship, the 'Mayflower'
in Plymouth Harbour, Boston, Massachusetts, U.S.A.*

*Monument in Wigan Lane, Wigan, commemorating the death of
Sir Thomas Tyldesley, who died in a battle fought there on the
21st August 1651.*

Duxbury Hall, Duxbury, Nr. Chorley, circa 1900.

Lodge house to Duxbury Hall, 2003.

Detail of the coat of arms of the Standishes of Duxbury contained in the lodge house. 2003.

The parish church of St.Wilfrid, Standish, existed in 1291 and was rebuilt in 1589 by Lawrence Shipway, the famous Elizabethan architect.

Elizabeth 1 was the last of the Tudor monarchs and on her death, on the 24th March 1603; James 1 succeeded her. There followed another period of religious persecution.

Myles Standish, described as " a son of the Isle of Man cadet branch of the house of Standish", had seen military service from shortly after 1600, with Queen Elizabeth 1 forces sent to the Netherlands to assist them with their fight against the Spanish. Myles Standish was a Puritan and, in an effort to escape religious persecution, obtained a charter from James 1 allowing a number them to colonise virgin lands in America.

In 1620, Captain Myles Standish with 101 others set sail in the 'Mayflower' from Plymouth bound for America. After enduring many hardships, a colony, known as New Plymouth, was set up in New England. Part of the colony was entitled Duxbury. This simple naming has been the cause of extensive research to establish properly the true origins and antecedents of Captain Myles Standish.

Civil War broke out in England and Scotland on the 22nd August 1642, when King Charles 1 raised his standard at Nottingham. Local sympathy lay mostly with the king. Ralph Standish of Standish had two sons who fought on the Royalist side, whilst Edward, the eldest son of Thomas Standish of Duxbury, was killed fighting with the Royalist forces of Lord Derby at Manchester in 1642.

24

Parliamentary forces also had their local adherents. Richard, the third son of Thomas Standish of Duxbury, inherited the estate on the death of his father in 1642. He subsequently became the leading Parliamentarian in the Wigan and Chorley districts, and was a colonel in their army.

King Charles1 was eventually put on trial for waging war on his own people. He refused to acknowledge the court, which sentenced him to death. He was publicly executed outside Whitehall Palace on the 30th January 1649.

The last battle of the Civil War in Lancashire took place in Wigan Lane, between Wigan and Standish, during 1651. Sir Thomas Tyldesley, a famous Royalist Major General, was killed in the fighting. A monument was erected to his memory by his Cornet (the lowest grade of commissioned officer in the cavalry), Alexander Rigby; and can still be seen on what was the site of the battle.

Hostilities came to an end when the Parliamentary troops accepted the surrender of Dunnottar Castle in May 1652.

Royalist sympathisers were severely punished following the Civil War. The Hornby family; the Norrises of Adlington; Edward Prescott of Standish; John Houghton of Park Hall; Hugh Pilkington and James Rigby of Coppull; William Anderton of Anderton and Thomas Langtree of Langtree; all forfeited their lands.

Ralph Standish avoided prosecution for involvement in the Civil War when Oliver Cromwell stayed a legal suit against him in 1653. Ralph died in 1665. His son, Edward subsequently purchased all the forfeited lands in Standish Manor during 1670.

There was always a close connection between the Earls of Derby and the Manor of Standish. At the siege of Lathom House in 1644, Edward Chisnall of Coppull distinguished himself in its defence.

James Stanley, the 7th Earl of Derby, was known as Lord Strange until he succeeded to the earldom following the death of his father on the 29th September 1642. At the outbreak of the Civil War he supported Charles 1. His plan was to secure Lancashire and raise troops there but the King is said to have been jealous of his royal lineage and commanded his presence at Nottingham. After several defeats the earl fled to the Isle of Man to escape the Parliamentary forces. He returned in 1644 and took part in Prince Rupert's successful campaign in the north of England. The siege of Lathom House, near Ormskirk was relieved and Bolton Castle was taken but following defeat at the Battle of Marston Moor, he once more fled to the Isle of Man.

On August 15th 1651 James Stanley landed at Wyre Water in Lancashire to support the King. The Royalist forces proceeded south but were comprehensively defeated in Wigan on the 25th August 1651. James Stanley managed to escape, despite being wounded, and joined the King at Worcester. However, he was captured near Nantwich, Cheshire, and tried by court-martial at Chester on the 29th September 1651. He received the death penalty. Despite appeals for a pardon and an unsuccessful attempt to escape, the earl was finally executed at Bolton in Lancashire on the 15th October 1651. He is buried at Ormskirk Church.

Charles 11 was restored to the English throne following the disputes and wrangling consequent upon

Cromwell's death. He was crowned on the 23rd April 1661, and reigned for a quarter of a century until his death on the 6th February 1685. His successor, James 11, was an avowed Roman Catholic, who was determined to place both Roman Catholics and Protestant Dissenters on an equal footing with his Anglican subjects. The result was failure and he fled the country, surrendering the throne to his son-in-law, William 111, in 1688.

Lancashire Jacobites plotted for the restoration of James 11 to the English throne. The cause divided many families including the Standishes. William Standish of Standish Hall was a zealot in the cause of King James, and the isolated position of the hall leant itself to the organisation of plots. On the other hand, Sir Richard Standish, the head of the Duxbury branch, was an active Protestant leader and busied himself in seeking out the plotters and bringing them to justice. There are many interesting stories involving Standish Hall in the conspiracy to restore James 11 to the English throne.

On the death of William Standish in 1705, his son, Ralph, inherited the estates. He too was a Jacobite sympathiser and joined the 1715 rebellion to place the son of James 11 on the English throne. The Scottish army was soundly defeated by government troops at Preston, and the leaders, including Ralph Standish, surrendered.

Despite being convicted and sentenced to death, Ralph Standish was eventually pardoned. His lands, which had been confiscated and sold, were re-purchased for him by the Duke of Norfolk and the Dowager Lady Petrie. On Ralph's death in 1755, Standish Manor and other estates went to his daughter, Cecilia, the wife of William Towneley. She held the manor until 1778, and is reputed to have founded the fair at Standish.

Edward Towneley Standish, the second son of Cecilia, became lord of Standish Manor in 1778. He died, without issue, in 1807. Edward's sister, Cecilia, married Charles Strickland of Sizergh, Westmorland, and their son, Thomas, inherited the Standish, Borwick and other estates. Incidentally, George Washington, (1732-1799), the first American President, was descended from the female side of this family.

Cecilia Strickland outlived her husband and subsequently married his cousin, George Edward Strickland. She died in 1814. Thomas Strickland Standish married Anastasia, the daughter of Sir John Lawson of Brough. His son, Charles Strickland Standish, inherited the manor of Standish but dropped the name Strickland.

Charles Standish married Emmeline Contradine de Mathieson. He led an esteemed life, being appointed Deputy Lieutenant for the County of Lancaster, and Member of Parliament (Whig) for Wigan. He gave up residence at Standish and travelled abroad extensively. He was the last member of the Standish family to live at the hall.

Standish Hall was, thereafter, leased to a succession of tenants until the death of the last member of this noble line, Henry Noailles Widdrington Standish. He was born in 1847, the only son of Charles Henry Lionel Widdrington Standish, by his wife, Angelique Leontine Sabine de Noailles. In 1870 he married Helene, daughter of the Count de Cars, and inherited the Standish estate in 1883 on the death of his father. He died at Contrexeville, France, on the 31st July 1920.

THE FACE OF SIZERGH CASTLE

The castle, which incorporates a fourteenth-century pele tower, has been given to the National Trust. It is described elsewhere on this page.

Newspaper extracts concerning the Strickland family's gift of Sizergh Castle to the National Trust in 1949.

700 YEARS

Mr. and the Hon. Mrs. Hornyold-Strickland, with their son, Lieutenant-Commander T. Hornyold-Strickland, are making a gift to the National Trust of the Sizergh estate, Westmorland, and other adjoining land, together with the contents of the castle. Owing to the increasing pressure of taxation they feel that the chances of the family's being able to retain possession in generations to come as it has done for the last 700 years are increasingly remote.

They are anxious that a house and estate to which a considerable archaeological and historical interest attaches shall not suffer the fate falling to-day on so very many properties, with the possible decay of one of the few remaining Border pele towers still occupied by the direct descendants of the original founders.

Sizergh—the name is of Norse origin denoting the dairy farm of one Sigarith—was granted by Henry II in about 1170 to the Deincourt family, while the Stricklands were living since the middle of the twelfth century at their manor of Great Strickland in the north of Westmorland. It was not until 1239 that the two families were allied by marriage.

PELE TOWER

The pele tower which forms the oldest part of the existing residence was erected in the fourteenth century. The windows of the topmost storey are of that date, and of special interest is the coat of arms and crest carved in stone below the top window seen from the courtyard recording the Deincourt-Strickland alliance. The house was first enlarged by the addition of a Tudor great hall, the original entrance on the east side and the fireplace being still untouched. The hall was first altered in the time of Queen Elizabeth when it was enlarged by a stone flight of stairs to a first floor level. Later, in the eighteenth century, it was considerably altered both inside and outside, a second floor was added, the windows changed at several dates, and the three-gabled roof converted into the present battlemented frontage.

Within the thick walls of the pele tower and in the unaltered centre-gabled block are panelled rooms in varying patterns, with some fine old wood and plaster ceilings, Tudor arched fireplaces and overmantels richly carved with figures and armorial designs. The beautiful room, since 1891 in the Victoria and Albert Museum, known as the Inlaid Chamber, came from the second floor of the pele tower, but it was fortunately found impossible to remove the ceiling of moulded plasterwork and frieze, the originals of which are still in place at Sizergh.

The pictures, most of which are family portraits, include good examples by Romney, Lely, Dobson, Kneller, Opie, Mary Beale, J. Ferneley, Downman, J. Allen, and others.

MALE DESCENT

During the 600-odd years since the Strickland-Deincourt alliance Sizergh has descended through the male line producing knights of the shire or members in 31 Parliaments, and filling the office of the shrievalty on 11 occasions. Generation by generation the family has fought in the defence of the Border and in the wars of the Crown oversea. One member bore the banner of St. George at Agincourt. At the revolution in 1688 the family followed the Stuarts into a voluntary exile of many years in France.

The last direct male descendant of the family was elevated to the peerage of the United Kingdom in 1926 for services in many parts of the Empire.

The family will continue to reside at Sizergh as tenants of the National Trust, and by mutual arrangement will open the castle and grounds to the public for a fee on certain days.

Local Links With The Howard Family.

The marriage this week in London of the Duke of Norfolk, head of the leading noble Roman Catholic family in the realm, who, as premier Duke and Earl Marshal of England, will be responsible for this year's Coronation arrangements, recalls that the Howard family, of which he is the representative, has interesting links with the Wigan district that may be appropriately referred to at this time. A marriage that greatly interested the people of Lancashire, and of the Wigan district particularly, was that of Ralph Standish, of Standish Hall, and Lady Philippa Howard, daughter of Henry, Duke of Norfolk, in 1698. The Standishes, like the Howards, were prominent Catholics, and Ralph Standish's activity in the Jacobite plots of the seventeenth century, as the Rev. T. C. Porteus points out in his "History of the Parish of Standish," was prophetic of the part that he played in November, 1715, when with a few servants and tenants he joined the Scots army at Preston. After the surrender he was taken to London for trial, and in the following January he wrote to his mother complaining of the severity of his imprisonment, and thanking her for her kindness to his children. In June he was placed at the bar and pleaded not guilty, the indictment being that he was with a great number of rebels and traitors at Preston on 12th November, 1715, to depose the King and exalt the person who took upon himself the title of James the Third. Ralph Standish was convicted and sentenced to death, but, chiefly through the influence of the Howard family, he was reprieved and liberated, and his estates, which had been seized and sold, were bought back on behalf of the family.

"W.O." ——— 30·1·37·

Norfolk Medals Left As Standish Heirlooms.

A year before Ralph Standish married Lady Philippa Howard family settlements were made in which Lord George Howard and Lady Philippa Howard took part, and also a little earlier when tithes of grain, wool, and lands in Standish, Shevington and elsewhere were claimed, the advowson of Standish Church being also included. When Ralph Standish was taken to London for trial Lady Philippa followed him to solicit her friends and relatives in his interests. Lady Philippa, it may be added, died seventeen years later, in 1732, and was buried at Standish. Ralph Standish's son took the name of Ralph Standish Howard, and he went to London and was patronised by Thomas, Duke of Norfolk. Many of Ralph Standish Howard's letters relating to his visits to London are preserved with the Standish Papers in the Wigan Library. Ralph Standish, who died in 1755, and, like his wife, Lady Philippa, was buried at Standish, left all his medals and curiosities, formerly belonging to the Norfolk family, to be enjoyed with Standish Hall as heirlooms. It is interesting also, in this connection, to mention that Lord George Howard by will, in 1720, left George, the son of Ralph Standish, a reversionary interest in property at Glossop.

The Rev. T. C. Porteus informs us that the Duke's family have had relationship with this district. In 1698 Ralph Standish of Standish Hall married Lady Phillipa Howard, daughter of Henry, Duke of Norfolk. Ralph Standish was a Jacobite, and took part in the rising of 1715. He was captured at Preston with brother officers of the Jacobite army and condemned to death. He was, however, afterwards reprieved and pardoned through the influence of the Howard family. This is referred to in Mr. Porteus's History of Standish.

Chorley Guardian 30·1·37

Another link with Lancashire was the marriage of Mary, daughter and sole heiress of Sir Nicholas Shirebourne of Stoneyhurst, Lord of the Manor and a moiety of Chorley, to the eighth Duke of Norfolk. As a Roman Catholic he registered his estates in 1718, these including lands in Chorley. In the possession of the Chorley Corporation is a map of the lands in and around the town in 1734, on which is described land as the estate of the Dowager Duchess of Norfolk, Mary Shireburne.

Sizergh Castle and Estate for the Nation.

Sizergh Castle, near Kendal, home of the Strickland family for the past 700 years, and one of the most historic buildings in the North-West, has been given to the National Trust. It is the first time the Trust has acquired a large historic house in this part of England. The gift has come to the Trust from the owners, Mr. and the Honourable Mrs. Hornyold-Strickland, with their son, Lieut.-Commander T. Hornyold-Strickland, and it includes Sizergh estate, other adjoining land, and the contents of the Castle. The family will continue to reside at Sizergh as tenants of the National Trust, and, by mutual arrangement, will open the castle and grounds to the public for a fee on certain days. Sizergh—the name is of Norse origin—was granted by Henry II in about 1170 to the Deincourt family, the Stricklands then living at Great Strickland in North Westmorland. The families were united by marriage in 1239, and a coat of arms and crest carved in stone on the building records this alliance.

"W.O." 15·10·49

A Strickland became M.P. for Wigan.

During the centuries since the Strickland-Deincourt alliance, Sizergh has produced Knights of the Shire or members in 31 Parliaments and filled the office of High Sheriff on eleven occasions. The last male descendant of the family was elevated to the peerage as Lord Strickland in 1926 for service in many parts of the Empire. The Standish family, of Standish Hall, intermarried with the Stricklands, of Sizergh, the Standish arms being afterwards quartered with those of Strickland, and later a Strickland succeeded to the Standish estates and became Whig M.P. for Wigan.

The Strickland of Sizergh who became Whig M.P. for Wigan.

22·10·49

In these notes last week, describing the gift of Sizergh Castle, near Kendal, the home of the Strickland family for the past 700 years, to the National Trust, it was mentioned that the Standish family intermarried with the Stricklands, of Sizergh, the Standish arms being thereafter quartered with those of Strickland. It was also added that later a Strickland succeeded to the Standish estates and became Whig M.P. for Wigan. In amplification of this, it is interesting to recall that following the intermarriage the name of Strickland appeared frequently in the Standish family nomenclature. When in 1807 Edward Towneley Standish died without issue Thomas Strickland of Sizergh, his sister's son, inherited the manor of Standish and assumed the name of Standish. His son, Charles Strickland Standish, who succeeded to the Standish Hall estates, was elected M.P. for Wigan in 1837 and also in 1842, and previously, in 1817, he was appointed Deputy Lieutenant of the county. Travel abroad and inherent good taste, it is recorded, had given him "most finished manners." His integrity and hospitality were highly praised, and his only offence in the eyes of his opponents was "that he is a Whig." He died in 1863 and was buried at Standish Church in the family vault. His eldest son, Charles Henry Widdrington Lionel Standish, who succeeded him, married Angelique de Noailles, and their son, Henry Noailles Widdrington Standish, died at Contrexeville, France, in 1920, without issue and with him the long ancestral line of the Standish family came to an end. His widow, Madame Standish, presented the Standish family muniments to the Wigan Public Library in memory of her husband, and as a token of the long connection between his family and the locality.

29

Strickland House, circa 1921.

Strickland House Farm, previously Strickland House. Photograph taken 2003.

LOT 51.

(Coloured Pink on Plan).

The Very Attractive
Gentleman's Residence & Pleasure Farm

KNOWN AS

Strickland House

WITH

66a. 2r. 7p.

of Excellent Agricultural Land.

SCHEDULE

Ordnance Enclosure.	Acreage.
611	.230
613	.328
612	.523
401	.565
332	5.655
335	1.656
331	5.110 (this includes .096 acres of Wigan Coal & Iron Co.'s optional lands).
330	.272 (ditto .019 ditto).
287	6.255 („ .644 „).
286	6.350 (House and Grounds).
285	19.981
281	9.384
279	7.368
280	2.867
	66.544

THE TIMBER on this Lot is valued at £260 which shall be paid for in addition to the purchase money.

THE HOUSE is substantially built of brick and slate with bay windows, and is of a very pleasant elevation.

It affords the following accommodation :—

GROUND FLOOR. Hall, Lounge Hall, Study, Fine Billiard Room, School Room, Morning Room, Drawing Room, Dining Room, Kitchen, Small Kitchen, Scullery, Larder, Cellar.

FIRST FLOOR. 9 Excellent Bedrooms, 2 Servants' Bedrooms, W.C's., 2 Bathrooms and Lavatories, Box Room.

Gas and water laid on.

THE GROUNDS are well kept and very ornamental. The Glass Houses comprise a Vinery and 4 Green Houses. There is a walled-in Kitchen Garden.

THE OUTBUILDINGS comprise, 4-stall Stable, 2 loose Boxes, Harness Room, Motor House for 2 Cars, Coach House and Wood House. In the Courtyard are Laundry and a large range of Store Houses.

The whole is very conveniently situated and screened from public view and is approached by a private drive known as "Beech Walk," skirted by well grown timber with Entrance Gate and Lodge suitable for a chauffeur's or gardener's cottage.

Early possession could by arrangement be obtained.

A right of way is reserved for the purchasers of Standish Hall and land adjacent over the road known as "Beech Walk."

The Wigan Coal and Iron Co. have a right of way along roadway 330.

This lot is let to Mr. W. H. Hewlett, a yearly tenant.

OUTGOINGS.—Tithe Rent Charge (apportioned sum) £8 19s. 1d.

Details of Strickland House, contained in the sales catalogue for Standish Hall Estate, 1921.

THE PARISH CHURCH OF ST. WILFRID, STANDISH

Sir Nikolaus Pevsner (1902-1983), the famous writer on art and architecture, refers to Standish Church as - "the most important church of the Elizabethan Age". He describes the building as - "entirely perpendicular (i.e. English Gothic architecture) except for the rather illiterate west steeple with its octagonal top stage, which dates from 1867".

According to Reverend Porteus, the church, dedicated to St. Wilfrid, is first mentioned in Hilary Term, 1205, in a dispute concerning "the last presentation in the time of peace". Alexander de Standish was Rector in 1206.

Little remains of the building that existed prior to the 16th century. A description of the church in 1544 finds it "in grete ruyne and decaye". Orders were then given for re-edifying it under heavy penalties for non-compliance. There are records of monies bequeathed for re-building in 1539, 1557 and 1558.

Richard Moody was instituted as Rector of Standish Church in 1559. He entered into an agreement in October 1582 for the re-building of the church. However, it is not thought that a total rebuild was necessary but, rather, a final effort to complete the work that had been underway for several years previously.

Projects undertaken during the restoration included the construction of the whole of the present nave and aisles, south porch and the greater part of the chancel. The old tower, which was square below and octagonal above, with an embattled parapet and spire, was left standing until 1867. The spire rising from the tower was, however, struck by lightning in 1814, and finally blown down during a violent storm in 1822.

Reverend Moody died in 1586 during the re-building of the church. Inevitably, there are conflicting accounts of the dates during which the re-building took place. The Victoria County History contains the following comment, "Whatever the exact date of the re-building, however, it appears to have been completed by about 1585, (Vol.6, page 183). Reverend Porteus puts the date of completion as 1589.

When the church was finally completed a number of questions arose as to whether the building should be re-consecrated as a new church, or it should continue to exercise all previous rights and privileges. Edward Standish, Patron of the church, sought Counsel's opinion on the matter, sometime after 1603. The outcome was that the church remained as previously but whilst the Patron was entitled to a key to the door of the chancel, the Parish Clerk should retain possession of the keys to the outer doors.

Several descriptions of Standish Church exist including a detailed account in the Victoria County History of Lancashire, (Volume.6, page 183), which reads as follows - "The church is built of local grit-stone in even and regular courses, but at the eastern end of the north side and in some other parts there are fragments of yellow and red sandstone, probably remnants from the earlier building. The walls throughout have embattled parapets, and the roofs, which are of very flat pitch and therefore not seen, are covered with lead.

Market Place, Standish, circa 1900.
'Spite Row' with the spire of Standish Church behind.

33

Exterior views of Standish Parish Church taken between 1900 and 1915.

Entrance to Standish church from Market Place, circa 1900.

View of Standish church from the graveyard, cira 1910.

The new church vestry shortly after it was built in 1913.

Interior view of Standish Parish Church, circa 1900.

Standish Parish Church interior, circa 1900.

The walls of the nave and chancel are continuous and of the same height, the division being marked externally only by octagonal staircases rising on either side as turrets with stone domed tops above the roofs. The aisles of the nave and chancel are also continuous and externally without distinction of division. The nave and chancel are lofty, with a continuous range of wide four-light clearstory windows with four-centred heads, and the line of battlement is varied by a wider merlon surmounted by a pinnacle over the middle clearstory window of the chancel, the second and fourth windows of the nave and over the east chancel window. The parapets on the east end of the north and south aisle are differently treated, that on the north side being stepped, while on the south the line follows the flat pitch of the lean-to roof. All the tracery of the windows is modern, of late Gothic character, with apparently little or no attempt to carry out the original design. The jambs and pointed heads of the windows, however, are original".

Reverend T.C.Porteus included the following passages in his 'History of Standish' - "Standish Church is remarkable for its height, spaciousness and beautiful proportions. The combination of late Gothic and Renaissance in the details is harmonious, and the limited use of the latter style does not spoil the general result. The church has the quiet dignity and charm of a mediaeval building, and is one of the most interesting parish churches in Lancashire" (Pages 53/54).

"NAVE - The nave of Standish Church is divided from the north and south aisles by arcades of five pointed arches, eleven feet wide, of two round chamfered orders, the label mouldings ending in shields. The arches spring from round columns with square bases, which are a yard high. The circular piers are of Renaissance style, with moulded caps and bases, beneath the four corners of the square abacus which surmounts the cap are round ornaments" (Page 65).

Many alterations, restorations and additions have been made to the church over the years. A new east window was installed in the chancel in 1799. The reredos, communion rail and chancel seats were installed in 1850, and further work carried out to the east window. A stove-heater was used in 1817, and gas lighting was installed in 1875. Harold Sumner Esq., of Ashfield House, Standish, gifted a new and larger church organ in 1913. Spacious new vestries for the clergy and choir, extending the entire width of the church, were built adjoining the east wall in 1913 and dedicated in April 1914. The churchyard was extended by a grant of land from E.T.Standish in 1805. Further land was consecrated in 1854, when the lych gate was also constructed. A Peace Memorial Gate inscribed with the names of members of the church who fell in the Great War, 1914-1918, was erected by public subscription, and unveiled on the 2nd October 1926.

Inside the church are many interesting memorials.

The Market cross, Standish, circa 1900.

Old Time Picture of Standish Parish Church.

31.1.31

Photo by   S. Richardson, Gathurst.

INTERIOR VIEW SHOWING GALLERIES.

The photograph shows a view of the interior of Standish Parish Church, as it appeared in the olden time. It will be noticed that there were galleries on three sides, and that the organ was in the gallery at the west end of the Church. About 1859 the galleries were removed, and the organ placed in the chancel.

The Wigan Observer

WIGAN, OCTOBER 22nd, 1949.

A Standish Helmet of Historic Interest.

The Standishes, of course, played a prominent part in history for centuries, and in this connection it may be noted that recently at Standish Church there has been brought to notice a medieval bowl-shaped helmet, or sallet, of a type which, being very rare, is exciting great interest among historians of armour. Last year it was borrowed by Captain Blair, a young Lancashire antiquary who is specialising in the study of the ancient armour of Lancashire and Cheshire, and was exhibited to a meeting of the Lancashire and Cheshire Antiquarian Society. The attention of Sir James G. Mann, the Keeper of the King's Armouries in the Tower of London, has been drawn to the Standish helmet, and he expressed a great desire to see it, with the consent of the Standish Church Council. The helmet is again being borrowed, and Captain Blair is taking it to London for exhibition at a meeting of the Society of Antiquaries on 17th November at Burlington House, when Sir James Mann will describe its interesting features. It is thought that the helmet belonged to a member of the Standish family of Standish Hall, probably the famous Sir Alexander Standish, who won renown in the Scottish Wars and was knighted by Lord Stanley in 1482 on the Hutton Field, receiving his knighthood from King Henry VII for his services, and also being granted an annuity for life from the revenues of the Duchy of Lancaster. Sir Alexander died in 1507, holding the manor of Standish and other possessions. When the Standish helmet, after exhibition in London, returns to the Church where it has for so long remained in oblivion, it will rank as an exhibit of historic importance and of national interest.

26.11.49

Historic Standish Helmet Lost and Found.

The fifteenth-century helmet, or sallet, which has reposed in the Standish Parish Church for centuries, and was described in these notes recently, has had quite a modern adventure. The helmet has excited great interest among historians of armour, and, at the request of Sir James Mann, Master of the Armouries at the Tower of London, it was taken to London for exhibition at a meeting of the Society of Antiquaries at Burlington House, on Thursday last week. After exhibition the helmet and other pieces of antique armour were taken from a Manchester Corporation bus on Saturday, when they were being brought from London. They were contained in a valise which mysteriously disappeared from the bus. Mr. C. Blair, a Lancashire antiquary, whose home is at Chorlton-cum-Hardy, who had charge of the valise, placed it under the stairs of the bus and sat where he could see it. In Oxford-road, Manchester, there was a crowd of people getting on and off the bus, and when they had cleared the valise with its contents had gone. A reward was offered for information leading to its recovery, and Mr. Blair appealed in particular for the return of the helmet. The loss was published in the Press, and, strange but happily to relate, helmet and armour were found next day on the railway in the Wigan district.

Part of Knightly Accoutrements in Medieval Days.

The helmet must have figured in exciting and colourful adventures when it formed part of knightly accoutrements in medieval days. It is thought to have been worn by the famous Sir Alexander Standish, of Standish Hall, a warrior renowned in the Scottish wars who was knighted on the field of battle in 1482. The circumstances in which the helmet vanished in 1949 were much more prosaic. From the rush hour of the Manchester bus traffic the scene moved to the quiet of Platt Bridge junction where a railwayman going home from work at 6.15 on Sunday morning discovered the valise and helmet lying near the metals, having apparently been flung from the train, and they were restored to Captain Blair by the Railway Police the following day. This week-end the historic helmet will be restored to the authorities of Standish Parish Church, where it will be once again placed back on the bracket, which it has occupied for generations. It is believed that there are only ten other examples of this type of helmet to be found in churches in England.

Newspaper extracts concerning the galleries in Standish church, and the Standish helmet.

37

Dean of Westminster's Lancashire Family Associations.

The Dean of Westminster, the Very Rev. William Foxley Norris, who has died this week at the age of seventy-eight, belonged to an ancient Lancashire family that is linked up with the Wigan district in an interesting manner. Dr. Foxley Norris, who was one of the most interesting personalities in the Church life of his generation, was the head of the Norris family of Speke, near Liverpool, and the family came into possession of the Speke estate in the fourteenth century, acquiring it by the marriage of William Norris, of Sutton and Blackrod, with Joan, heiress of Sir John Molyneux, of Sefton, and they held it until the beginning of the nineteenth century when the dissipation of the family fortunes necessitated its sale. The Norris family, of Blackrod, and the Bradshaigh family, of Haigh, inter-married, and Dame Mabel Bradshaigh, who gave her name to Mab's Cross, Standishgate, and was the heroine of the Mab's Cross legend, was a member of the Norris family, being the daughter and sole heiress of Hugh Norris "de Haighe and Blackrod." The recumbent marble figures of Lady Mabel and her husband, Sir William Bradshaigh, whose long absence at the wars occasioned the romance that is bound up with Mab's Cross, repose in the Wigan Parish Church. Sir Walter Scott founded his novel, "The Betrothed," on the romantic story of Dame Mabel Bradshaigh and her absent knightly husband who, when presumed to be dead, returned unexpectedly in the habit of a pilgrim, and slew his rival. Sir Walter Scott mentions that Mab's Cross was standing in 1832 when he dated his novel from Abbotsford. In this connection it is interesting to recall that the Cross remained on the west side of Standishgate until 1919, when it was demolished for road widening purposes and re-erected on the other side of the road by an archæological expert, Lord Crawford, as head of the House of Haigh, defraying the cost. A water colour painting of Mab's Cross, by John Ralston, as it appeared at the time of the publication of "The Betrothed," hangs on the walls of the Wigan Public Library.

Shevington Poor Boy Who Became A Rich Shipper.

When the Speke estate, which has been so prominent in the news recently in connection with the establishing of the air-port there, was sold by the Norris family, it was purchased by Richard Watt, a wealthy Liverpool merchant and shipper, who was once a poor boy at Shevington, and the family which he founded lived at Speke Hall until a few years ago. When Miss Adelaide Watt, the last representative of the family, died, the property, by the terms of her will, passed to the present-day descendants of the Norris family, of whom the Dean of Westminster was one. In Standish Parish Church there is a handsomely carved marble monument to Richard Watt, the self-made merchant, who purchased the Speke estate from the Norris family, and the Rev. T. C. Porteus gives a fine full-page illustration of this monument in his "History of Standish." Richard Watt, who died in 1796, was born in 1724 at Shevington of a poor family, and his arms and crest, with several emblems of commerce, appear on his monument in Standish Church. In Smither's "Liverpool," published in 1825, Richard Watt is commended as an example of successful industry. His master, Geoffrey Whalley, sent him to an evening school, and eventually he went to Jamaica and acquired a large fortune. On his return to England, after an absence of forty years, one of his first acts was to seek out and provide for the survivors of his former employer's family. He built the mansion called Oak Hill, at Old Swan, Liverpool, and also purchased the manor of Speke. The estate descended to Miss Adelaide Watt, who gave £1,250 for a Bishop's Throne in Liverpool Cathedral in memory of Richard Watt, the poor Shevington boy who became the rich Liverpool shipper.

Standish Parish Church contains this sculptured memorial to Richard Watt, of Oak Hill and Speke Hall, Liverpool, who died in 1796.

ELIZABETHAN MANSION FOR LIVERPOOL

FROM OUR CORRESPONDENT *1943*

LIVERPOOL, July 28

Liverpool City Council to-day approved a proposal to lease Speke Hall with 35 acres of grounds, for 99 years at a nominal rent from the National Trust and to buy 125 acres of agricultural land and woods around the hall for £6,000.

The Deputy Lord Mayor, Sir Sydney Jones, said the acquisition would add greatly to the city's amenities and give it closer contact with the past. It was a joy that the city would now have this hall, which was the only Elizabethan black and white timber mansion built around a quadrangle.

The Trust is to arrange for most of the hall's contents, including armour, ancient weapons, furniture, and tapestry to remain there.

SPEKE HALL ESTATE
28.7.43
LEASE FROM NATIONAL TRUST APPROVED

The leasing to Liverpool Corporation of Speke Hall and its 35 acres of grounds for 99 years from the National Trust, and the purchase of 125 acres of agricultural land and woods surrounding the hall, for £6,000, were recommended by the Finance and General Purposes Committee at to-day's meeting of the Liverpool City Council.

The Council approved.

Alderman Sir Sydney Jones said this acquisition would add greatly to the amenities of the city and give it closer contact with the past.

He congratulated Alderman Shennan on the manner in which he had carried through the negotiations with the National Trust, and also expressed his appreciation of the part played by the Finance Committee and members of the Council. They owed thanks, too, to the National Trust.

It was a joy to him that Liverpool would now have this beautiful hall, which was the only Elizabethan black and white timber mansion built round a quadrangle.

Contemporary newspaper cuttings relating to the life of Richard Watt, and the lease of Speke Hall and estate, from the National Trust to Liverpool Corporation, in 1943.

Wrightington Hall, showing the Tudor section which was demolished in 1929, at which time two Priest's cells were found, which confirm the use of the hall for Catholicism during the Reformation period.

These two views of Wrightington Hall, and the head office, were taken circa 1930.

Wrightington Hall was incorporated into Wrightington Hospital, seen here in 1960.

Main entrance to Wrightington Hospital, circa 1930.

The marble altar tomb of Sir Edward Wrightington lies on the south side of the chancel in Standish Church with his effigy lying on top. He was a member of the Council of the North, and died in 1658. Hugh Dicconson, his heir, was responsible for the erection of the monument.

16th CENTURY REBUILDING OF STANDISH CHURCH.

8·9·28

INTERESTING LETTER OF RECTOR MOODY WRITTEN IN 1565.

FOUND AMONG WRIGHTINGTON HALL DOCUMENTS.

Amongst the Wrightington Hall documents recently placed in the charge of the Wigan Library Committee by Colonel Gerard, there has been found a letter written by Rector Richard Moody, of Standish, in 1565, acknowledging a contribution to the rebuilding of Standish Church and Mr. J. M. Ainscough, J.P., of Lindley Mount, Parbold, has sent us the following transcript of this interesting document, with its archaic spelling:—

"Thys Bill made the XVth daye of July in the seventh yere of the Reigne of oure Sovran Ladye Elizabeth, by the Grace of God Quene of England, France and Irelande, Defender of the Faith, witnessith whereas Thomas Wrightington, John Wrightington, Richard Wrightington, esqiers, of theyr gudnes dyd giffe to the Buyldynge of the p'isshe Church of Standishe the sum of thre ponds of current money of England wherefore by thes be it knowin that Margaret late wiffe and Execut'x to the said Ric. Wrightington hath payd the daye hereof unto the hands of Sir Ric Modie, p'ist, Peter Standishe and Roger Beseley, the townshippe, for the towne or hamlet of Standishe the said sum of thre ponds to the use of the said Church. First XLVI shillings and VIIId. thereof to be payd for a berne and XIII shillings and IVd. the reversion of the said III ponds to be bestowed towards a Table beying the cheiffist and the beste instruments for the buyldynge of the said Church. Therefore we, the said Ric Modie, Peter Standishe, and Roger Beseley, by thes presents do nott only acknowledge to have receyved the said sum of III ponds to the use of the Church as is said but also by thys Bill of aquittance do hereby aquyte and discharge the said Margaret Wrightington and hyr executors thereof forever. In the recorde herof to thes presents we, the saide Ric Modie, Peter Standishe and Roger Beseley have sealed and signed and putte oure hands the daye and yere aforesaid.
　　　　by me Richard Modie,
　　　　　　Rectour de Standyshe."

The letter is written on a sheet of strong, handmade paper, measuring 12 inches by 8 inches, and the ink is as fresh to-day as the day it was written.

Mrs. Wrightington to whom it was addressed was buried in the chancel of Standish Church on 6th December, 1580, her husband, Richard Wrightington, having been buried in the same vault seventeen years previously, in 1563, which, as will be noted, was two years before the writing of the letter.

Rector Moody, the writer of the letter, who was Rector of Standish for a period of twenty-eight years, died in 1586, during the rebuilding of the church, to which he had very largely contributed.

Colonel Gerard of Wrightington Hall presented documents relating to the estate, to Wigan Library Committee in 1928. Amongst these was information in a local newspaper cutting concerning the re-building of Standish Church, which is included.

View of Standish Parish Church from the graveyard, circa 1920.

The entrance door to Standish Parish Church, above which can be seen the stone carving of an open-bible and the ancient sundial clock. The stone sarcophagus was excavated from the north-east corner of the church, where the first or foundation stone is traditionally laid, and where the founder was sometimes buried. 2003.

A view taken from the older part of the graveyard. 2003.

This large boulder was discovered at a depth of 11 feet by H.T.Cottle, the Parish Clerk, on the 14th September 1895, during renovation works and presently stands near to the entrance door of the church. Alongside it is the stone sarcophagus.

A commemorative stone tablet records the building of the church vestry in 1913. The text reads, "Anno Salutis Reparatae 1913. This vestry was erected for the use of the church and to the happy memory of Annie Rose Hutton by her brother, John T. Adams, Snaithfield, Ecclesall, Sheffield: By her sister, Mary Adams, Patron of the Benefice: And by her husband, C.W.N.Hutton. M.A., Rector. Gloria Tibi Domine".

The entrance doorways to Standish Parish Church are varied and differ in age and design.

In the wall which presently divides the churchyard from the Parish Centre (built in 1999), can be seen these carved stones, which were once part of the old church.

The pulpit, lectern and reredos at Standish Parish Church are visible, with the memorial tablets above the pulpit 2003.

The memorial tablets above the pulpit are monuments to the Worthington family, incorporating the date 1584, and to Thomas Clayton of Adlington, who died in 1722.

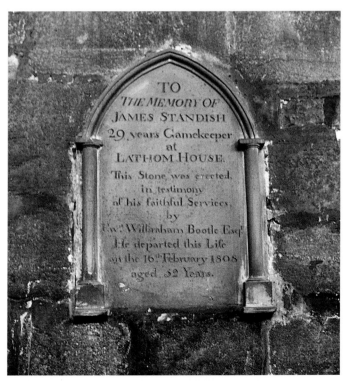

A stone memorial to James Standish who was the gamekeeper at Lathom House, Near Ormskirk, for 29 years, and who died on the 16th February 1808.

The elaborate marble monument was erected in memory of Edward Chisnall of Chisnall in Coppull, and records his bravery at the siege of Lathom House. He died in 1653. Below is an enamelled brass plate dedicated to the memory of Canon William Harper Brandreth, M.A., who was instituted on the 26th June 1841, and died on the 17th April 1885.

Reverend Richard Perryn, M.A., was instituted as Rector of Standish Parish Church on the 10th May 1779. He is described as "one of the most active and industrious rectors that the benefice has known". He was involved in a variety of commercial activities including growing willows for basket makers, providing oak bark for the tanners, and selling apricots, potatoes, meal, timber, clay and sand from the rectory and glebe. Rev. Perryn maintained meticulous records, which still survive and have proved most useful in providing information of the times he lived through. He had a special interest in education being credited with the foundation of several educational establishments in the district, including the National Schools at Adlington and Shevington. He died at Trafford Hall, near Chester, on the 31st October 1825, aged 72 years, and is buried at Thornton-le-Moors Church. The congregation and parishioners of Standish Church contributed to the erection of the memorial.

Cecillae Towneley, daughter of Ralph Standish, and wife of William Towneley of Towneley, who died in 1778, is commemorated on this tablet. Reference is also made to her son, Edward Towneley Standish, who died in 1807.

On the north side of the chancel is the tomb of Richard Moody who was instituted to Standish Rectory on the 3rd January 1558 (or 1559). He was in office during the re-building of the church but did not see its completion. His death occurred in November 1586 and he was buried in Standish Church. There has been much debate concerning the effigy of a parish priest on top of the tomb.

John and Ellen Hodson of Ellerbeck Hall, who both died in 1828, are commemorated on this marble monument, erected by their nephew and heir, Reverend Richard Cardwell.

There are many old gravestones providing evidence of the age of the church. This particular monument, dated 1696, is situated against the outside vestry wall, although it has most probably been removed from its original position. The stone adjacent to it dates from 1621 and is the oldest one known in the graveyard.

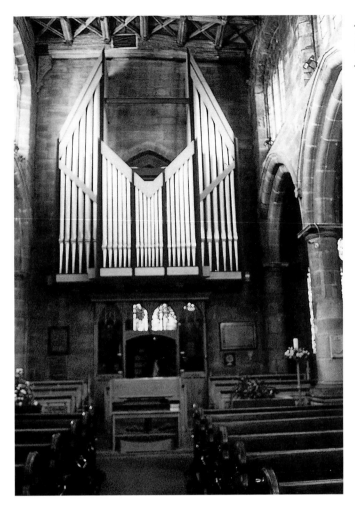

An organ was first installed in Standish Parish Church during 1843, the cost of about £400 being raised by public subscription. The present organ was the gift of Mr. and Mrs. H. Sumner of Ashfield House, Standish, in 1913.

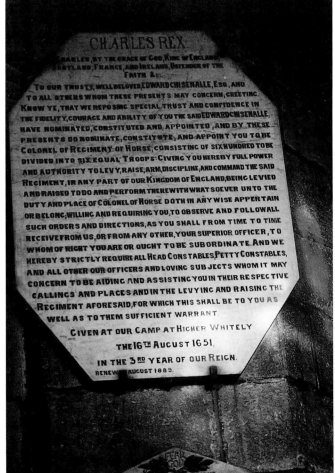

There was formerly a marble tablet in the church, which recorded two commissions awarded to Edward Chisnall, by Prince Rupert and Charles 11, respectively. This was replaced in August 1889, by the memorial, shown.

Standish Church roof was constructed in the 16th century rebuilding of the church. It is comprised of moulded and ornamented principal oak beams, with two moulded cross beams, which with ridge and purlins, form a section between two principals consisting of 18 square panels. These are boarded and crossed by diagonal moulded ribs, in saltire fashion, with carved bosses at the intersections.

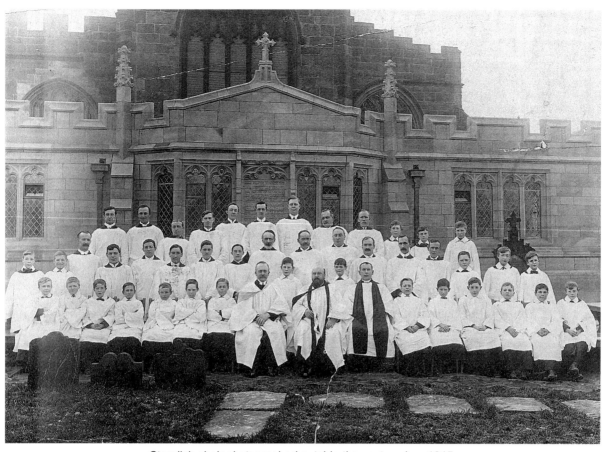

Standish choir photographed outside the vestry, circa 1915.

Standish church choir with a trophy awarded for competition singing.

STANDISH RECTORY

Rectors of Standish Parish Church have long enjoyed rights and privileges over vast tracts of land in the parish. Reverend Porteus comments that, "The lords of Standish and Langtree agreed in 1284 that the rector should have the waste of land and wood between his arable field fence and Southbrook in length, and between Ruleclough below Worthington, Swacroft and Wallclough, in breadth. (Later the width was between Kilnclough and Wallclough). He was to have also, as before, the Stockhey (a field near Rectory Farm still called by that name), and it should be lawful for him to make assarts. He also had entry to the common pasture and wood of Standish and the pasture of Langtree".

The parsonage for the incumbent at Standish Church was described as being in a ruinous state during 1535, and was re-built by Bishop Henry Standish. Four years later, in 1539, the parsonage was leased to Reverend Peter Bradshagh, a condition being that, "he was to have meat, drink and lodgings, for himself two servants, and their horses, when he came to his parsonage, and the lessee was to keep hospitality there".

Parsonage, or Rectory Farm, was included in the glebe properties, along with Lark Hill, Bessie's Well Farm, Town Farm, Moody House, and numerous fields. The 'Black Horse Inn' stood near to Moody House, on glebe land. It was removed and re-built in 1804, and two dwellings were erected on the site in 1807.

Standish Rectory was re-built in 1887 by the Reverend (later Canon) Charles William Newton Hutton, M.A. He was educated at St. John's College, Cambridge, and was instituted at Standish Parish Church in 1886. Reverend Hutton was in office at the time that Reverend Porteus completed his 'History of Standish'. Among the many benefactions made to the church during the time that Reverend Hutton was the incumbent, are the provision of memorial shields on the chancel screen, the founding of a church library of historical books, and the construction of the church vestries which were dedicated in 1914.

Reverend Hutton was an excellent organiser and hosted many functions in the spacious and well kept grounds of Standish Rectory. He left the benefice in 1938, and was succeeded by Reverend Walter Samuel Mellor.

Bryn Mount, Wigan Road, Standish, was purchased in August 1943, to be used as a vicarage. The property was eventually sold in 1965, to provide funding for the construction of a completely new rectory, opposite the lych gate of Standish Church, in Rectory Lane.

The old rectory, which had been re-built by Reverend Hutton, was subsequently demolished and the 'Owls Restaurant' presently occupies the site.

Field days on the extensive lawns at Standish Rectory, circa 1900.

Standish hand-bell ringers outside the Rectory, circa 1910.

Standish Rectory

Close-up view of the Rectory, circa 1920.

Standish Rectory Lodge House, 2003.

Letter written by Reverend Hutton, to Father Walmesley at St. Marie's Church, on the 1st May 1914.

May 1. 1914

Dear Father Walmesley,

Many thanks for looking up the point about Bishop Dicenson. I have been frequently asked & could give no reply. The in partibus rather mislead me. I was looking for it as some missionary see, possibly now slipped from memory. No doubt Bishop Dicenson occupied an important position & the name of his see was a secondary matter. Curiously enough I had a visit - also from Father Cook about the same time & he has also replied confirming what you say. Many thanks.

Yours very sincerely

Reverend C.W.N.Hutton, with his sister Marion outside the rectory in 1936.

Ernest and Sarah Ellen Birchall, who resided at the Rectory Lodge, circa 1918.

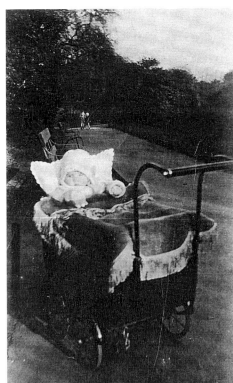

Mr. and Mrs. Birchall, had one son, Cyril, who is pictured here in the grounds of the rectory and in choir boy's outfit.

St. Wilfrid's Parish Church, Standish, 31st August 1957. Cyril Birchall is pictured with his wife, Alice, and their two children, Alan and Eric, attending a wedding at the church.

The Owls of Standish, Restaurant, which was built on the site of the old Rectory, 2003.

Rear view of The Owls, Rectory Lane, Standish, 2003.

St. Wilfrid's House, which stands next to what was Standish Girls' School, circa 1925.

Reverend Charles Edward Bramley,
Rector of Standish Parish Church from 1956 until 1980.

The Old Rectory, Wigan Road, Standish, 2003.

The present day rectory for Standish Parish Church, which is situated in Rectory Lane, opposite the lych-gate, 2003.

ST. WILFRID'S PARISH CHURCH WALKING DAYS

Processions of witness were a popular event, particularly for the children. They provided an opportunity to sport ones best clothes and enjoy the celebrations. The camera was much in evidence during walking days, when both amateur and professional photographers recorded the scenes. It was mainly the congregation of the Church of England who took part in street processions of witness, along with the Methodists. Roman Catholics tended to confine their walks to the vicinity of their own church. Old walking day views, like topographical street scenes, are extremely interesting because of the amount of local history which can be gleaned from them. Several of the older views date from the beginning of the twentieth century and the tramway system is clearly visible on a number of them. Among the later scenes, are a series of four photographs, taken near St. Wilfrid's church in the 1930's, and one of Shevington Walking Day taken about 1950.

Procession of Witness in High Street, Standish, circa 1905.

The Wheatsheaf public house, which stood on the corner of School Lane and Preston Road, is on the extreme left of this post card photograph taken about 1905.

St. Wilfrid's Jubilee Banner, obtained in 1897 to commemorate Queen Victoria's Diamond Jubilee of her 60 years reign, is being carried, along with another banner relating to Captain Myles Standish, circa 1905.

A solitary policeman heads the procession near to the top of Church Street, Standish, circa 1905.

The procession takes up the full width of High Street, Standish, on this view taken circa 1910.

These four walking day photographs were taken in the vicinity of St. Wilfrid's church, in the 1930's.

Shevington walking day, circa 1952.

CATHOLICISM IN THE STANDISH DISTRICT

Reverend Father A. Walmesley of St. Marie's Church, Standish, wrote a brief account of the Catholic history of Standish and neighbourhood for the 25th anniversary of the church in 1908. A fund raising Bazaar was held from the 4th to the 7th November 1908, and the account was published in a souvenir handbook sold in connection with the event. The purpose of the Bazaar was to raise funds to reduce some of the capital debt on the Church and Schools, Presbytery and Parochial Rooms.

Father Walmesley's historical account is very interesting and I have relied on it for some detail of this section.

In 325 A.D., Constantine the Great, who was the son of the Roman Governor of Britain, Constantius Chlorus, and who was born at York, became the first Christian Emperor of Rome. He was converted to Christianity by a miraculous vision of the Cross of Christ in the sky, with the motto, "In this sign shalt thou conquer".

Pope Gregory the Great sent St. Augustine, together with forty Benedictine monks, to England in 596 A.D., to spread Christianity. The mission proved largely successful as within a century the whole of England was converted.

Some time after the Battle of Chester in 613 A.D, the Standish district became dependent on the see of York.

Wilfrid, Bishop of York dedicated his new church at Ripon about 675 A.D. Northumbrian Kings gave certain holy places, abandoned by the clergy of the defeated Britons, to the see of York. These included a number between the Rivers Ribble and Mersey. Standish Parish Church is dedicated to St. Wilfrid but this does not necessarily determine the date of its foundation because an existing title may have been altered.

The Norman Conquest did not alter the religion of England, which remained Catholic until 1534.

King Henry V111 wanted to secure a divorce from Queen Catharine, in order to marry Lady Ann Boleyn in 1530. He sought the help of Pope Clement V11 but was denied assistance, and in consequence declared himself Head of both State and Church in 1534.

At this time, the Parish Church of St. Wilfrid at Standish had four altars on which the holy sacrifice was offered daily.

1. The altar of Our Lady's Chantry, in the present chancel, founded in 1328 by the parish priest Sir Henry Le Waleys or Walsch. At this altar, thirteen lights were to burn before the Blessed Sacrament on every holy-day forever. In Edward V1's time, the last priest of this Chantry, Rev. William Bymeson, was dismissed with a pension.

2. Over the chancel threshold, and reached by a flight of steps, stood the Rood Altar, founded about 1483, by James Standish Esquire of Duxbury. The priest of this Chantry also, the Rev. Peter Bower, was dismissed with a pension.

3. On the north east side of the Chancel stood the Altar of St, Nicholas, founded about 1470 by the Rector, the Rev. Alexander Fairclough, of which Chantry, so far as appears to be known, the Rev. James Nevore was the last mass-priest.

4. To the north west of the Chancel stood, most probably, the Chantry Altar of the Standishes of Standish, kept always in their own hands as a private foundation.

Henry V111 died on the 28th January 1547, and was succeeded by his son, Edward, born of his third wife, Jane Seymour, on the 12th October 1537. Edward V1 was therefore 10 years old on taking the English throne. Despite constitutional arrangements to cater for this circumstance, the new King's uncle, Edward Seymour, Earl of Hertford, seized power. He established himself as Protector of the realm and sole guardian of the King. He took the title, Duke of Somerset, and proceeded to make England a Protestant State. The Catholic Act of Six Articles passed into law in 1539, was repealed, the Chantries were abolished, and an English prayer book was issued in 1549, largely compiled by Thomas Cramner.

The destruction or defacement of altars, relics, chalices, church books, crucifixes, images, stained glass, and pictured walls was ordered, which meant that Catholicism could now only be followed in secret. Several local halls were used for this purpose, including Standish Hall, Langtree Hall, Blainscough Hall, Park Hall, Burgh Hall and Worthington Hall.

A number of sacred antiquities were in fact saved from destruction and preserved in the Standish Mission. These included a chasuble and stole (priest's vestments), and the sacring-bell used at Mass.

In the reign of Mary 1 (1553 - 1558), the Catholic religion was publicly restored. New altars were speedily erected and England was formally re-united with the Roman See of Peter. However, on Mary's death on the 17th November 1558, Elizabeth 1 succeeded to the throne. She became Supreme Head of the Church and enforced allegiance from her subjects on pain of death.

Reverend Richard Moody (Moodie), who was formerly a monk of the dissolved Franciscan House in Friargate, Preston, became Pastor of Standish Church on the 3rd January 1558 (or 1559). Despite his appointment as a Church of England Rector, he remained at heart a Roman Catholic until the end of his life and hoped for a future Catholic sovereign.

Near to the altar in Standish Church is a tomb with the full-length figure of a Franciscan monk on top. His hands are raised in prayer. An inscription reads, "Here lies Richard Moodie who, for 38 years, was the very vigilant pastor of Standish Church. He, at his own expense, provided food for the surveyors and masons at the building of this temple, which twice suffered ruin".

Standish Hall was re-built in 1574 to replace an existing manor house, and the new structure contained a Chapel for Mass. One of the first priests to minister at the hall was Father Laurence Vaux. In October 1559, Father Vaux left his position as Warden of Manchester College to escape the Queen's

Commissioners. He took with him the College deeds and muniments, church-plate and vestments; a large portion of which he secretly deposited at Standish Hall.

Father Vaux was in virtual exile and spent much of his time in Louvain, Belgium, returning occasionally to England. All the Catholic bishops were eventually imprisoned and Father Vaux undertook a dangerous trip to England to help the aged Bishop of St.Asaph, Doctor Goldwell, to give the Sacrament of Confirmation. Unfortunately, Father Vaux's presence in England was betrayed and he was imprisoned for treason. He died in Clink Prison, Southwark, in 1585.

The Blessed Edmund Campion preached at Blainscough, Coppull, then Standish Hall, before making his way to London to receive the Crown of Martyrdom on the 1st December 1581.

Father Edward Bamber was captured at Standish Hall in 1643 and detained at Lancaster Castle. After three years in prison, he was tried for his life. Two witnesses against him, described as fallen Catholics, named Malden and Osbaldestone, attested that they had seen him administer the Sacraments of Baptism and Matrimony. He was found guilty and the death penalty was imposed on either the 6th or 7th day of August 1646.

King Charles 11 became a Catholic on his deathbed, receiving the Sacrament from Father Huddlestone, who 30 year earlier had concealed him after the Battle of Worcester. On the succession of James 11 some liberty was once again afforded to his Catholic subjects. He only reigned for four years however, finally giving up the throne in favour of William 111, who was merciless in his persecution of Catholics.

In 1694, Government agents informed the King of a conspiracy, allegedly centred at Standish Hall in Lancashire. Caryl Lord Molineux, Sir Wm. Gerard, Sir Rowland Stanley, Sir Thomas Clifton, William Standish, Bartholomew Walmesley, William Dicconson and Philip Langton, Esquires, along with Wm. Blundell, junior, gentleman; sought the restoration of James 11 to the English throne.

William Standish managed to escape and a reward of £500 was offered for his capture. The remaining eight conspirators were to be tried for treason at Manchester in 1694. It is said that their death warrants had been signed even before the trial began.

Juliana Dicconson of Wrightington, wife of William Dicconson, was Bartholomew Walmesley's sister. A Protestant friend informed Juliana, in confidence, that the evidence against the alleged plotters had been fabricated by paying informers to give perjured evidence. The purpose behind the prosecution was to execute the principal Catholic gentry in Lancashire and confiscate their estates.

Lunt and Company of London were involved in the prosecution along with Aaron Smith. Juliana Dicconson, in order to protect her brother, secured an interview with the company, ostensibly to provide damning proof of the guilt of the accused persons. Her brother-in-law, Roger Dicconson, disguised himself as a Mr.Howard, and supplied totally fictitious information to aid the prosecution case.

During the trial of the alleged conspirators at the Autumn Assizes in Manchester, the principal prosecution witness, Mr. Howard, did not turn up. The whole charade of a trial finally disintegrated when Roger Dicconson gave evidence for the defence. He revealed his own identity and the villainous purpose of the prosecution. The jury immediately acquitted the accused men. The witnesses who gave false evidence were pelted out of Manchester and Aaron Smith was lucky to escape with his life.

Squire William Standish died on the 8th June 1705 and was succeeded by his son, Ralph Standish, who married Lady Philippa Howard, daughter of Henry, Duke of Norfolk. Ralph was involved in the Jacobite uprising of 1715, being taken prisoner at Preston. In spite of being sentenced to death for treason, he was subsequently reprieved.

When the Catholic Emancipation Act, 1829, became law, Catholic chapels, schools and colleges were once more allowed, and the priests no longer needed to disguise themselves or work in secrecy.

The Standish family built the Hermitage as a presbytery. A Sunday school and night classes were also conducted there for children to receive both religious and secular instruction.

A Catholic day school was operated in 1865 from a cottage known as Cat i'th Window. Efforts by Father Corlett resulted in a senior school being built in 1869, the foundation stone for which was jointly laid by Mrs. Frances Taylor of Strickland House, Standish, and Miss Cecilia Walmesley.

By 1883 the old chapel at Standish Hall was proving too small for the growing congregation and the present St. Marie's Church was built. Mr. Henry Standish made a gift of the site for the church, and made a generous donation towards the cost of building and the provision of a graveyard. The foundation stone for the church was laid on the 24th June 1883. The church was completed and opened for worship by the Bishop of Liverpool, Dr. O'Reilly, on the 18th May 1884.

A Presbytery and Meeting Room were also built on the site, near to the church, and were completed in 1908. The Standish family, further assisted by extending the priest's tenure on the Hermitage until the presbytery was built, and contributing towards the cost of the two additional buildings.

Copy of correspondence between Henry N.W. Standish, the owner of Standish Estate, and Father John Barry, parish priest at St. Marie's church from 1873 to 1893, offering assistance for the building of a church.

Paris. 12 Jan. 1883 –

37, Rue Dumont d'Urville.

My dear Father Barry

I have heard from Mr. Witham of his interview with you and as my great desire is and always has been to satisfy you. and to make the most beneficial arrangements for the Catholics at Standish

I have great pleasure

in stating what I undertake will be agreable to you – I will contribute £500 towards the erection of a new church or chapel to be built near the Site suggested when I was last at Standish and the precise position of which Mr. Collingwood will arrange with you I will make a present of that Site to the Trustees of the Diocese, but I or other, the possessor

for the time being of Standish (being a Catholic) must always be one of the Trustees. I will also instruct Mr. Collingwood to supply sufficient timber (as far as practicable) off the Estate in order to assist in the building I should of course like to see plans & estimates of the proposed Church I understand that in consideration of my

contributing £500 as above mentioned you are prepared to guarantee £1000 more towards the erection and I hope and fully believe that if necessary you will be able to obtain other contributions from Catholics in the neighbourhood –

I shall be happy to allow you to continue at the Hermitage and I will go on paying you as heretofore that

68

37, Rue Dumont d'Urville

is £50 a year, £30
salary and £20 for
Chapel expenses and
I will allow you coals —
Should I (which I do
not anticipate) have
occasion for the Services
I would find you some
Suitable residence —
Of course as I continue
these payments I shall

consider you still as
my chaplain and
Should I come to live
at the Hall, I should
expect you to arrange
to Say mass when
necessary in my private
Chapel which I should
in all probability
build at the Hall —
You will of course
understand that I do

not intend handing
over the Hermitage
to the Mission —
I do not object to your
having a Cemetery
by the Church provided
it is kept out of Sight
as much as possible.
Hoping to hear Soon
from you on this Subject
Believe me,
Yrs respectfully & truly
Henry Stanish

EXTRACTS FROM FR. WALMSLEY'S DIARY.

1897. OCT.11th. Teaparty & Entertainment (to pay for new Senior classroom which had been added to school in 1896)

Stage erected previous Wednesday evening by Messrs T. Ashton, L. Foster, R. Danson etc. Saturday I got J. Heyes to cart tea-tables and legs, tea-urns, and short church forms for infant school. With John Hagan, fixed tables. On Monday at 9½, Heyes carted the hams and beef etc. Altar boys carried lamps down and candlesticks and candles, and took tickets out.
Carvers at 10. Mrs Clarkson, J. Foster, Baldwin, Annie Ball, Mary Gerrard, Ann Hilton, A. Ashton...Mr. H. Ball and Mr. John Foster. Mr. Abbott late at lamps.
Tray Holders. Ball, Gerrard, Ashton, Clarkson, Baldwin, Hooton.
Had 100 chairs and 2 rows forms in front.
Best produced so far. Tambourine Drill and songs, 16 girls. Mrs. Willis's Will (Lizzie Whelan and Maggie Fairhurst danced) Darkies, Choir.
Larger attendance...two fine nights. Children..about 330 at tea and 20 mothers in Infants School. Total in at Entertainment..400 (40 on stage).

1908. Sunday, JAN. 12th. Extract from Fr. Walsh's notes for first meeting for Sale of Work. 6.30 p.m. School.
Now 24 years since ceiling of venerable Chapel fell (1884), and warned pastor not only too small, but too old for further use........
In 1883 Mr. Standish (Henry) presented the site of new church and presbytery, and gave £500. Without his only continual help no priest without private income could have carried on the mission without going into bankruptcy.
The reduced contract for shell of church is £3230.
Then the heating apparatus, benching, altars, pulpit etc. about £4,000.
Wall round graveyard £555. Architect, £180.
No clerk of works, for economy's sake. Hence about £600 by Dean Barry and myself in repairs.
Owing to great cost of Church, Mr. Standish lengthened the Priest's tenure of the Hermitage. That will finally cease 15months hence at the latest.
About 2 years ago, (1906) I negotiated with the Bishop and Mr. Standish re a Presbytery and meeting room. Mr. Standish promised £250. Bishop inserted another Confessional.
Mr. Birrell's Education Bill delayed the project, for we should need all we had for Schools, and I intended to give all I had to pay salaries of teachers. On the defeat of that Bill I immediately resumed preparations.
When the plans were completed and approved by Bishop, it was found that the shell of the buildings proposed could not be completed for less than £2,300 exclusive of architect and Clerk of Works, gas fittings and heating apparatus.
It was then a question whether the parochial rooms and the new confessional should be postponed until the presbytery should be paid for.
Eventually, with Bishop's approbation I took on myself the responsibility if necessary, for £1,000, not immediately but if I live a few years and remain here. Already paid £555 which will no doubt have to come out of my own patrimony.
Have here plans for heating new buildings from present boiler, which will be enlarged. First estimate £133, cut down to £76 £86.
Hot-pipe heat a cheerles, brain deadening heat. Hence only half the warming will be by pipes.
Open fire-place in the assembly room, in reading room, and in billiard room.

Extracts from Father Walmsley's diary.

St. Marie's of the Annunciation
STANDISH.

ON SUNDAY, JUNE 24, 1883,
THE

FOUNDATION STONE
OF THE
NEW CHURCH
WAS
SOLEMNLY BLESSED & LAID
BY
His Lordship the Bishop of Liverpoool.

Extract from a letter of His Lordship the Bishop, written from Aix-les-Bains on May 13.

"My dear Fr. Barry,—I have been anxious to know what has been done or is doing about your New Church. I hope to be home in a few weeks, and it would be a real joy to have to visit Standish to bless the foundations. I hope you are getting substantial help. With best wishes, I am, my dear Fr. Barry, very faithfully yours, ✠ BERNARD O'REILLY."

During the building of the Church there will be a Weekly Mass for all Subscribers.

N.B.—The New Church will probably be ready for opening early in 1884. A BAZAAR will be held previously to the opening, and Fr. BARRY will feel most grateful for any contributions in aid of the same.

Programme for the laying of the foundation stone at St. Marie's Church.

Detail of the foundation stone for St. Marie's church, dated 24th June 1883.

St. Marie, Our Lady Of The Annunciation church, photographed circa 1900.

Interior view of St. Marie's church, circa 1900.

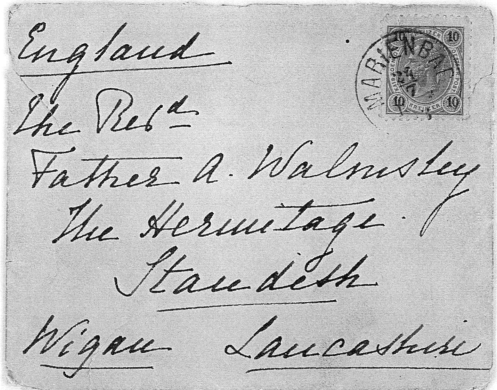

Copies of correspondence, dated 1893, between H.N.W.Standish, and the parish priests of St. Marie's church who resided at the Hermitage, Father John Barry and Father Alfred Walmsley.

Paris 26 June 1893

43, Avenue d'Iéna

My dear Father Barry

I received yesterday your very kind letter but I cannot say how very sorry I was to read the contents of it — I am grieved more than I can say to think that you are going to leave Standish where you have done so much good for the last twenty years, but I quite understand that it is hard work for you & I think that you cannot refuse the appointment at Chorley which is offered to you by the Bishop — It would be selfish of me to induce you to remain at Standish. The only thing I beg of you is to find out who the Bishop is going to name in your place as it will be so difficult to replace you in every way — of course you can tell the Bishop that I will be very willing to give your successor the same help to salary &c.

I have been very poorly lately & I am going this evening to Marienb to take the waters.

It would be most kind of you to write to me there & tell me your plans & when you think of leaving. I cannot think of not finding you at Standish when I shall go there in the autumn.

Many thanks for writing to me about all this & with kindest regards

Believe me

Yours very respectfully & sincerely

Henry Standish

Goethe Haus
Marienbad
Austria. 24th July 1893

Dear Father Walmsley

I was very glad to receive your letter & to hear that you had been named successor of Father Barry. I sincerely hope you will like Standish & I feel sure you will take a great interest in the mission — you cannot do better than follow Father Barry's footprints in every way as he has been an admirable priest I must repeat to you that I shall be very glad to continue the allowance I gave to Father Barry and it will be a great pleasure for me to make your acquaintance when I go to Standish in the autumn. Hoping that you will not forget both Mrs Standish & myself in your prayers & with kind regards.

Believe me dear Fr Walmsley yrs respectfully & truly.

Henry Standish

My address will be always.
43. Avenue d'Iéna
Paris

74

Father W.P.Corlett, parish priest at St. Marie's church, 1863 to 1872.

Father Alfred Walmsley, parish priest at St. Marie's church, 1893 to 1919.

Standish Hall

Fred. J. Barnish.

Etching of Standish Hall, by Fred J. Barnish, 1898.

The Hermitage, Standish, which for many years was used as the presbytery for Standish Hall.
When the new church of St. Marie was built in 1883, the Standish family allowed the continued use of the Hermitage
until the present presbytery was constructed in 1908.

The "Cat i'th' Window" at Standish

20.5.33

Photo by H. Parkes.

FAMOUS CATS OVERHAULED.

The house in the picture known as "Cat i'th' Window," which stands on the right hand side of the road which runs from Standish to Wrightington, has recently been re-decorated externally, and the famous cats re-painted on the wall. Though it is now really a modern building, this house dates back to the days of Oliver Cromwell. Originally it was a farm, with a fine thatched homestead, but it was burned down over thirty years ago, and has since been rebuilt. The front wall was left standing, and when finished the cats, which were supposed to be a dairyman's sign, were again painted on the building to keep up the tradition. There is a saying about this old house that William Standish, the Jacobite, hid there, while evading the law, and concealed himself in an old chest, with two compartments. When an officer searched the place he drove his sword through some linen in the chest, and went away. The fugitive escaped unhurt, and later was successful in fleeing to Holland.

The "Cat I'th' Window," Standish.

21.4.28

WHERE WILLIAM STANDISH, THE JACOBITE HID.

Photo by W. Hughes,

THE OLD THATCHED BUILDING THAT WAS BURNED DOWN.

People travelling from Standish to Wrightington may have noticed a cottage on the right-hand side of the road, with cats painted on the wall. This cottage is known as "Cat i'th' Window." Though it is now really a modern building, it dates back to the days of Oliver Cromwell. Originally it was a farm, with a fine thatched homestead, but it was burned down twenty-seven years ago, and has since been rebuilt. The front wall was left standing, and when finished the cats, which were supposed to be a dairyman's sign, were again painted on the building to keep up the tradition. There is a saying about this old house that William Standish, the Jacobite, hid there while evading the law, and concealed himself in an old chest with two compartments. When an officer searched the place he drove his sword through some linen in the chest, and went away. The fugitive escaped unhurt, and later was successful in fleeing to Holland. The photograph shows the cottage as a fine old thatched building thirty years ago before it was burned down.

Newspaper cuttings, relating to the Cat i'th' Window cottage, Almond Brook Road, Standish.

Interior of the church, circa 1920.

St. Marie's church and war memorial, showing its original position, circa 1925.

St. Marie's church, presbytery and schools, circa 1925.

Close up view of the war memorial.

Father James Norris (1920-1928) outside the entrance to St. Marie's church, circa 1925.

Interior of St. Marie's church, circa 1925.

Workers in St. Marie's church graveyard, circa 1930. They are (left to right) William Fairhurst, Frank Woodruff, Steven Hodcroft, Teddy Fairhurst and Jack Fairhurst.

Golden Jubilee celebrations for St. Marie's church, 1934.

Commemorative cup, issued for the 50th Anniversary of the opening of St. Marie's church, Standish.

St. Marie's church procession, 1935, with Canon Campion leading, followed by the children from Notre Dame Convent.

A procession took place in 1935 to celebrate the Silver Jubilee of King George V. The congregation of St. Marie's church was involved and can be seen with the church in the background.

Children of Mary procession, 1935.

Boys processing around St. Marie's church, 1953.

Celebrations were held in 1952, for Canon Campion's 40 years in the priesthood. He was the parish priest at St. Marie's from 1928 until 1959. He is pictured with colleagues.

The May procession, 1952.

Canon Campion in procession, circa 1950,

Canon Campion at the Corpus Christi procession in 1953

Members of St. Marie's church on their Pilgrimage trip to Lourdes, leaving from Earlestown railway station, 1963. Doctor Malone is accompanied by Alice Fairhurst, Molly Bullen, Margaret Cumberbatch, Nellie Grady, Bernard Woods, Cuthbert and Agnes Darwin, Harry Woods and IMrs. Woods. The remainder have not been identified.

STANDISH QUAKERS

George Fox (1624 - 1691) founded the Quaker movement in 1647, which he named 'The Society of Friends'. Whilst accepting the scriptures as God's word, he considered them to be of secondary importance because he felt that God communicated directly with his people. Therefore, he did not see the need for churches or ministers but accepted that a 'meeting place' could assist in bringing together those persons of a like mind.

Quakerism came to Coppull in the 1660's, a most difficult time when the restoration of Charles 11 to the English throne meant that all religious worship except that of the Church of England was prohibited.

William Gibson, a follower of George Fox and his beliefs, preached in the Standish district during the 1660's, and seems to have acquired Heskin Fell as a convert. Heskin Fell was born in Coppull on the 22nd July 1640, and carried on a trade as a linen weaver, employing a number of servants and apprentices.

The Haydock family were the tenants of the Perburn Estate, which lay on the boundary between Standish and Coppull. Hugh Haydock came into possession of the estate from his mother, Catherine, about 1512. She had inherited the property from John Perburn. The family residence was Perburn Hall or, as it later became known, Bogburn Hall.

William Haydock succeeded his father, Hugh, in ownership of the Perburn estate and was in turn followed by his son, Roger, who held the lands in 1598. In the same tradition, Roger left the estate to his son, John. Finally, in 1622, on the death of John Haydock, his son, also named Roger, inherited the lands.

Roger Haydock married Alice Nightingale, who held Presbyterian beliefs. The couple had five sons, John (born 1640), Roger (born 1643), William (born 1646), Henry (born 1655), and Robert (born 1660). They also had two daughters.

In 1652 Roger Haydock, obtained the lease of Langtree Hall, near Standish, due to the impoverishment of the Langtree family by the Civil War. Less than a mile away from Langtree Hall is Bogburn Hall or Perburn Hall, as it was previously known. This property was either built or re-built in 1663 by Roger Haydock.

Roger Haydock (senior) became interested in Quakerism, possibly due to his wife's Presbyterian leanings. Three of their sons, John, Roger and Robert, eventually became Quaker ministers. Another son, William, graduated with a Master of Arts degree from Cambridge University and was subsequently appointed as Rector of Standish Church.

John Haydock was 27 years old when he became a Quaker and devoted much of his life travelling to spread the faith. In April 1668, John attended a meeting at Bury together with his brother, Roger. Such a meeting was, at that time, illegal and was raided by the authorities. Both brothers were arrested and taken before Robert Holt, J.P., who committed them to Lancaster Prison to await trial. The reason for their immediate confinement was that they refused to supply a bond to appear before the Quarter Sessions. In the event, they remained incarcerated for three months, being released on the 28th July 1668.

Roger Haydock was 24 years old when he became a Quaker and travelled extensively throughout the British Isles, Holland and Germany, to preach his beliefs. Like his brother, John, he often suffered fine or imprisonment. John Haydock wrote a biography of his brother, Roger, following the latter's death in 1696. The comment is made that, "It is remarkable that, in all the itinerant preaching expeditions he undertook throughout England, he apparently escaped fine or imprisonment except when near home".

The only mention of all three of the Haydock brothers appears in the biography of Roger Haydock. In it we are told that on the 29th April 1696, Roger and Robert Haydock, with their wives, and brother John, went to Talk Hill in Staffordshire. The two ladies were then left with John who was going to take them to London, whilst his brothers returned home. On the 10th May 1696, Roger died following a sudden attack of 'malignant fever'. He was buried at the Friends Burial Ground, Grayston, near Penketh.

John Haydock was unable to attend his father's funeral in 1670 because he was preaching in Ireland. However, as the eldest son he inherited the estate. In 1679 John Haydock married Ellen Milner of Blyth in Nottinghamshire, the daughter of Gamaliel Milner, late of Burton Grange, near Barnsley.

The Government tended to view Nonconformists, including Quakers, as being suspect. Bogburn Hall was searched for arms in 1683 when there was suspicion of a plot against either the Government or King James 11.

John Haydock suffered many further terms of imprisonment whilst preaching his beliefs throughout the British Isles. He was accused of involvement in the Jacobite plot by supplying William Standish with arms. He refused to take the oath when giving evidence before the Commissioners of Rebellion. This was natural for a Quaker whose belief was that a simple 'yea' or 'nay' was sufficient. Further imprisonment was ordered although the term is unknown.

In 1719, John Haydock was again imprisoned at Lancaster. He was taken ill and died there. His body was returned to Coppull and interred at the Quaker burial ground at Langtree, Standish.

The first Quaker Meeting House was built on the burial ground site at Langtree in 1717, just two years before John Haydock's death. His son, also named John, registered the building at Ormskirk Quarter Sessions on the 2nd July 1717.

Armorial bearings of the Haydock family of Coppull and Standish.

The Quaker Meeting House, Langtree, which was demolished in 1904.

Bogburn Hall, Coppull, once the home of the Haydocks. The two date stones (shown on page 88) refer to Roger and Alice Haydock and John Haydock. Both bear the date 1663.

A

POSTSCRIPT.

MY Brother, about 1674, or 1675, being at a Meeting at *Freckleton* in the *Fylde*, in *Lancashire*, was apprehended and brought to *Preston*, before *Edward Rigby*, called Justice, who treated him very Roughly, and gave him many opprobrious Speeches, calling him, and one taken with him, *Traytors*, &c. and fined him 20 *l.* for Preaching. This said *Rigby* endeavoured to lay the Fine upon the Hearers; but my Brother told him, he had Goods of his own, better than 20 *l.* and therefore none ought to be imposed upon because of his Fine; *Rigby* said he would have them.

Several Years after, this same *Rigby*, with others, was, in King *James*'s time, apprehended and sent from *Preston* to *Chester*, by *Warrington*; at which place, neither at *Inn-houses* (many Soldiers being in Town) nor at private Houses, could they get Entertainment, until my Brother took this *Rigby*, and some others of

of them into his House, then other private Persons gave Entertainment to the rest. After this my Brother did go to *Chester*, and in Prison there, did visit this *Rigby* and the rest; so that after they were released, upon their return, this *Rigby* gave an Account how kind a *Quaker* had been, in giving him Entertainment, and Visiting him, &c. in Prison, whom he formerly had been so Unkind unto, and dealt so Unchristianly with: So that this my Brothers Hospitality to him (who exercised Cruelty when he had Power) in the time of his Distress, did demonstrate my Brother to be a true Follower of Christ, and one that had learned to do Good, and to extend Charity to such as had been Evil-minded, and greatly made their Cruelty manifest. This Account I received from Friends,

John Haydock.

Coppul, the 16th of the 2d Month, 1697.

F I N I S.

John Haydock wrote a biography of his brother, Roger, in 1697, and these two pages refer to Roger's kindness to Justice Edward Rigby, which was not deserved.

The site of the Quaker burial ground, Standish, recently refurbished by the Standish Community Forum.

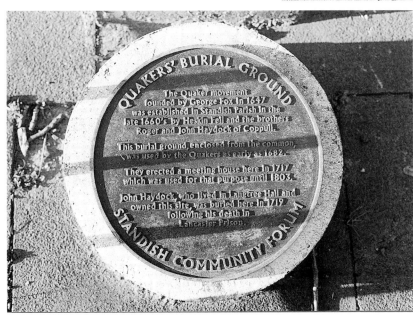

QUAKERS' BURIAL GROUND

The Quaker movement
founded by George Fox in 1647
was established in Standish Parish in the
late 1660's by Heskin Fell and the brothers
Roger and John Haydock of Coppull.

This burial ground, enclosed from the common,
was used by the Quakers as early as 1682.

They erected a meeting house here in 1717
which was used for that purpose until 1803.

John Haydock, who lived in Langtree Hall and
owned this site, was buried here in 1719
following his death in
Lancaster Prison.

STANDISH COMMUNITY FORUM

John Haydock (junior) later conveyed the burial ground and meeting house to his brother Joseph, whose daughter, Ellen, married Thomas Boardman of Manchester. They subsequently sold the lands to Mrs. Polly Penson of Wigan in 1813.

Standish Quaker Meeting House was used until 1803, when a new building was erected on land leased by the trustees of Standish Grammar School, and known as the School Croft. The old Meeting House was used as a cottage until it was demolished in 1904.

The Society of Friends in Standish remained small in number and gradually diminished after the deaths of the principal adherents, Heskin Fell and the Haydocks. Alexander Parkinson, who was born in 1701, assumed the mantle of principal Quaker for a while but only 29 followers are recorded in a census of the parish taken in 1764. The Meeting House at School Croft was eventually sold to a Mr. Brooks.

John Wesley preached Methodism in Standish about 1770 and attracted many converts. In 1850 the Wesleyans rented the ground floor of the Quaker Meeting House from Mr. Brooks but by 1858 were in a position to purchase the building outright.

Eventually the Methodists built their own Chapel in High Street, Standish, and moved there in 1897. The Meeting House was subsequently demolished.

A second Quaker Meeting House was built on what is now Quaker's Place, off School Lane, Standish.

Hic jacent Excuviæ
Venerabilis admodum Viri Domini Gulielmi Haydock
Qui per annos XXXVII
Ecclesiam hanc ornauit Rector Pastor emendauit
A Flectas Oculos Orientem Verfus
Per illum Altare cui Sacerdos.
Ufq ad vitæ Finem aftitit spectabis ornatius
Aly sua ad Altare ferant Dona
Hic noster Deo et Ecclefiæ donauit Altare
Monumentum sane illud Ære hoc perennius
Et quod hoc saxum immobile diu conferuabit
Quale autem Aures nostras ab occidente ferit melos
A ad Occidentem Te Convertas
Per Flumen nouæ Psalmodistis Extructæ sunt sedes
ut ab Oriente nempe ufq ad Occidentem
Ad Extremos Scilicet Mundi Terminos Fidei Catholicæ Dogmata
Et Harmonia Simul Evangelica Refonarent
Neruos Omnes intendebat Vir tam Pius quam Pacificus
Gregi Pastor fponfæ maritus Flebilis Occidit
Id April A Ætatis Suæ LXVII Salutis Noftræ MDCCXIII

A brass memorial plaque lies near to the altar in Standish Church. Eleanor Haydock of Bolton prepared the sketch of the plaque, which is included. A translation of the text reads as follows,

TRANSLATION

"Here lie the remains of the highly venerable man, Reverend William Haydock, who for 37 years honoured this church as Rector Pastor. So may you turn your eyes towards the east through that altar at which the priest, up to the end of his life stood. You will look at something quite adorned. Let others bear their gifts to the altar.

Here our man gave to God and to the church, the altar, that truly a memorial more enduring than this bronze, even because this immovable rock will long remain intact. Moreover, as a tune strikes our ears from the west, so may you turn to the west. Through the inspiration of the late singer of psalms, benches have been built so that from the east certainly to the west, indeed to the farthest ends of the world, the teachings of the catholic (universal) faith and at the same time the harmony of the Gospels may resound.

A man as pious as he was peace making, he stretched all his sinews as a shepherd to his flock. The husband of his weeping spouse died on the Ides (13th) of April at the age of 67, in the year of our deliverance, 1713".

The ruins of Guest Farm, Welch Whittle, once the home of the Haydock family.

American descendants of the Haydock family were responsible for the erection of this tablet to their memory in 1922.

METHODISM IN STANDISH

John Wesley is regarded as the Father of Methodism, and following his death on the 2nd March 1791, his diary was published by his adherents. There are a number of visits recorded in the area of Standish and one in particular reads as follows. We went to Wigan, for many years proverbially called Wicked Wigan: but it is not now what it was: the inhabitants in general have taken a softer mould. The house in the evening was more than filled; and all that could get in seemed greatly affected, while I strongly applied our Lord's words: "I will; be thou clean".

Despite the success of Wesley's teaching, not all the followers of Methodism were in total agreement with the new form of religion. Many felt that it was too near to that of the Church of England and preferred to be 'free' as the Nonconformists were.

Several secessions were created, one of them being the Primitive Methodist Church, founded in 1810, not long after John Wesley's death, by Hugh Bourne (1772-1852) and William Clowes (1780-1851).

Originally, Standish Methodists rented the ground floor of the Quaker Meeting House at Langtree, in 1850, being in a position to buy the building outright in 1858. A Primitive Methodist Chapel was built in Preston Road, Standish, during 1891, and a Wesleyan Methodist Chapel in High Street, Standish, during 1897. Both churches could accommodate 250 worshippers.

Eventually the various splinter groups, including the Primitive Methodists, re-united with the Wesleyan Methodists, principally because the latter retained the greatest following. This re-unification was completed by 1932.

Standish Primitive Methodist Church was finally demolished in the 1990's and services are now conducted at the Chapel in High Street.

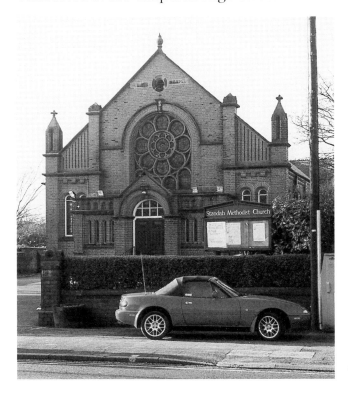

Standish Methodist church, High Street, Standish, 2003.

Standish Methodist church, High Street, Standish, circa 1920.

Standish Methodists ready for the walking day about 1960. Alan and Eric Birchall, David Ryder, Trevor Jones, Martin Kennedy and Christopher Pilkington are amongst the group.

Preston Road, Standish with Pole Street to the right, June 1964. The four young men at the front carrying the Methodist Church banner are (left to right) David Pilkington, Alan Birchall, Jim Jones and Michael Kennedy.

The Salvation Army

William Booth (1829-1912) founded the Salvation Army in 1865. Its mission has always been to the poorest members of society.

General Booth visited the Standish area in 1907 and this rare post card photograph of him was taken in High Street.

General W. Booth, founder of the Salvation Army, photographed on a visit to Standish in 1907.

JAMES MARTLAND AINSCOUGH
1854 - 1937

In July 1937, M.Margaret Ainscough of Lindley Mount, Parbold, completed a biography of her father, James Martland Ainscough (J.M.Ainscough) that was published by James Starr & Sons, Ltd., Dawber Street, Wigan. The assistance of the Reverend Thomas Cruddas Porteus, B.D., is acknowledged, along with others, in bringing the project to print.

The book is particularly interesting because of the information contained about Standish. Two lasting legacies for which J.M.Ainscough can be given credit are the preservation of the Standish family deeds and papers and enhancing the appearance of the Market Place in Standish. The contents of this interesting publication are summarised below.

The Ainscough family had local roots going back several generations. James Ainscough, the father of J.M.Ainscough, was born at Heskin in 1812. On his marriage to Sarah Martland of Wrightington, in 1853, the couple chose to live in Standish and purchased a house to the north side of Market Place.

Their matrimonial home had an interesting history. In 1755 it was the home of Mistress Mary Smalley, the niece of Reverend Edward Smalley of Standish Parish Church. She founded a School of Pious Learning and Useful Industry for twenty girls, which opened in 1797. The principal teacher was named 'Dolly' and the pupils wore uniforms consisting brown Coburg frocks, with tippets (woman's fur cape for the shoulders), poke bonnets, worsted stockings (knitted by themselves), and Blucher buckled shoes. Educational subjects taught at the school included spinning, weaving and winding thread for the weaving carried out in their respective homes. A special pew was reserved in Standish Church for the girls and they attended every Sunday with the principal. The combination of their distinctive dress and the fact that the principal was named 'Dolly' earned them the nickname 'Dolly's Chickens'. The school eventually became part of the National Schools.

James Ainscough farmed the land behind his home. In 1853 he cleared a row of old sycamore trees from the front of his property. Although farming was his main occupation he also acted as Overseer and Assessor of Taxes for the Township of Standish.

J.M.Ainscough was born at Standish on the 25th February 1854. He grew up in the area attending the Infant School in Rectory Lane, before going on to Standish Grammar School. Fees at the grammar school were 2d per week but they were doubled to 4d if Latin and Mathematics were taught. J.M.Ainscough studied the additional subjects.

'Spite Row', Market Place, Standish, circa 1900. The well, stocks and market cross can be seen in front of the houses. Apparently the lamp near the well was the focal point for local children to play in safety.

J. PENDLEBURY,

CRAWFORD HOUSE, WIGAN.

SHOW DAYS, WEDNESDAY, APRIL 14TH, AND FOLLOWING DAYS

NEW GOODS IN ALL DEPARTMENTS.

LATEST ESIGNS IN MANTLES, JACKETS, SKIRTS, SHAWLS, &c.

CHOICE SELECTION OF MILLINERY AT REASONABLE PRICES.

CHILDREN'S SUN HATS, BONNETS, MILLINERY, COSTUMES, CLOAKS, PELISSES,
FANCY APRONS, CORSETS, UNDERCLOTHING, &c., &c.

DRESS DEPARTMENT.

IN THE DRESS DEPARTMENT WILL BE FOUND A LARGE STOCK OF
FRENCH MERINOS, CASHMERES, NOVELTIES IN DRESS FABRICS, VELVETS,
VELVETEENS, PLUSHES, SATINS, &c.

Extraordinary value in Biege, 6½d. ; Kyrl Cloth, 11½d.

FANCY DEPARTMENT.

BUTTONS, GIMPS, FRINGES, LACES, SILK SQUARES, MUSLIN WORKS, COLLARS,
GLOVES, &c.

China Silk Squares shades, 12½d. ; French Kid Gloves, 16½d., 1s. 11½d.

MANCHESTER DEPARTMENT.

EW PRINTS, ZEPHYR GINGHAMS, QUILTS, TOILET COVERS, TOWELS, TABLE
CLOTHS, NAPKINS, &c.

New Zephyr Ginghams 4d. per yard.

CRAWFORD HOUSE, WIGAN.

105—7n

PENDLEBURY & AINSCOUGH,

CRAWFORD BUILDINGS,

STANDISHGATE, WIGAN.

CABINET MAKERS, UPHOLSTERERS, CARPET FACTORS, AND

GENERAL HOUSE FURNISHERS.

SOILED !!

☞ TO BE CLEARED OUT AT COST PRICE

A FEW

DINING and DRAWING-ROOM SUITES ; also SIDEBOARDS and

CABINETS to Match.

A Very Handsome DRAWING-ROOM SUITE, in Stamped Velvet, £8 10s. 0d. ;
CABINET to Match, £6 0s. 0d.

A Solid Oak DINING-ROOM SUITE, in Real Leather, £15 0s. 0d.
SIDEBOARD to Match, £6 15s. 0d.

A JOB LOT OF FANCY TABLES, from 5s. each.

Newspaper adverts from the Wigan Examiner dated the 24th July 1886.

James Martland Ainscough.

Example of a silver enamelled medallion presented to past mayors of the County Borough of Wigan.

Standish, as it appeared in the 1850's and 1860's, when J.M.Ainscough was a boy, is remembered with particular affection. It was a prosperous and picturesque village with quaint old thatched cottages in Church Street, Preston Road and in the Grove. These premises had lovely old-fashioned gardens. They were replaced with ugly rows of brick-built houses. The old Court House in Cross Street had a triangular green and a large overhanging beech tree in front. The Malt Kiln Pit once used by the local youths for skating in frosty conditions was subsequently filled in and the site used for the construction of a Wesleyan Chapel.

Market Place was the centre of village life in those days. Thomas Booth, the blacksmith, always attracted a crowd of children who would watch him work and an old war veteran, named Bibby, was fond of relating his exploits during the Peninsular War (1808 - 1814). Mrs. Cicely Strickland, the sister of Edward Townley Standish Esq., founded a cattle fair held annually on the 25th November - St. Cecilia's Day. A long established fair was also held on the 29th June each year, known as the Whitsuntide Fair. There were many in attendance to enjoy the swings and roundabouts, sideshows and the like.

On leaving school in 1869, at the age of fifteen, J.M.Ainscough was indentured as an apprentice to Mr. John Pendlebury, a draper in Standishgate, Wigan. He continued to pursue this trade with Messrs. Ray and Miles of Liverpool and Messrs. Denby and Spinks of Leeds. He eventually returned to the Wigan area and set up a furnishing business on his own account in Wigan.

A request from John Pendlebury, with whom J.M.Ainscough had served his apprenticeship, resulted in the two entering into a business partnership, trading as Pendlebury and Ainscough, from Crawford Buildings, Wigan.

In 1898, the drapery and furnishing departments were amalgamated and the concern became a private limited company, trading as Pendlebury and Company Limited. However, the death of John Pendlebury in December 1898, led to a further re-organisation with the company being registered as a public company, with J.M.Ainscough as its first Chairman and Managing Director.

Crawford Buildings were altered on several occasions to accommodate the expanding business. Even the recession experienced following the First World War (1914 - 1918) did not affect the firm too badly. Part of the company's success was its object to provide good quality and value for its customers.

Whilst retaining his position as Chairman of the Directors, J.M.Ainscough retired from business in 1924, then being 70 years of age. He remained involved with the company until the last days of his life.

Religion and public duty were important to J.M.Ainscough and he held positions as a manager at several local church schools including St.Catharine's and Whelley Schools. He was an active member of the local Conservative Association being involved with both the Wigan and Standish Conservative Clubs.

Following his appointment as a Magistrate for the Borough of Wigan on the 22nd August 1900, he held a number of important offices. Amongst them were Chairman of the Licensing Committee and a member of the Advisory Committee for the selection of Justices of the Peace for the County Borough of Wigan.

A plethora of other important public offices held by J.M.Ainscough saw him as Trustee of Wigan Savings Bank, Honorary Arbitrator of the Lancashire and Cheshire Miners' Permanent Relief Society and, during the Great War, he acted on the Wigan Tribunal.

After Prospect House, Standish, was destroyed by fire in 1910, J.M.Ainscough moved to live in Parbold. He was offered the Mayorality of Wigan in 1919 but had to decline because Mrs. Ainscough was seriously ill. However, he finally accepted the office in November 1922 and became the 676th Mayor of the Ancient and Loyal Borough of Wigan.

During his year of office, J.M.Ainscough steered the purchase of the Elms Estate for the Borough and prompted the inauguration of the War Memorial Fund. Wigan's War Memorial stands near to Wigan Parish Church. Sir Giles Gilbert Scott was responsible for the design of the memorial and the unveiling ceremony took place in October 1925, when Lieutenant General Sir Herbert Lawrence officiated. The memorial has been described as "one of the finest in the country".

On his last day as mayor (November 9th 1923) J.M.Ainscough wrote the word "ICHABOD" in his diary, a Hebrew word meaning "the glory is departed". A few days prior to the 9th November someone called at the Town Hall to see if the mayor was available to attend a function on the 9th. The mayor's attendant consulted the diary and being puzzled as to the meaning of the one word entry said, "The mayor must be going to one of those tin chapels up Lamberhead Green way"!

Antiquarian interests always fascinated J.M.Ainscough. He was a member of the Society for the Preservation of Ancient Monuments and joined the Lancashire and Cheshire Antiquarian Society in 1902.

In 1920, J. M.Ainscough invited his friend, Reverend T.C.Porteus, to accompany him to the Isle of Man where they would try to unravel the mystery of Captain Myles Standish's connection with the Standish district. On return a book containing their findings was published. Reverend Porteus wrote the History of Standish some seven years later.

Henry N.W.Standish, who was the last surviving member of that noble family, died in Contrexville, France, in 1920. The Standish estate was afterwards sold and the old hall was partially demolished.

Fortunately, the Deeds and Papers of the Standish family were secured by Wigan Corporation, chiefly due to the efforts of J.M.Ainscough.

The well, cross and stocks, Market Place, Standish, circa 1920.

Prospect Hill House was built on Grannum's Hey, Standish, in 1793. George Ainsley who was the steward for Standish Manor was in occupancy during 1806. It was the home of James Martland Ainscough from 1893 until it was destroyed by fire in 1910. Following the re-building, it was tenanted by Arthur Leach. During the First World War the property was used to house Belgian refugees. Latterly, the residence was used as a care home for the elderly but it is now empty and boarded up to prevent vandalism.

The date stone of Prospect Hill House contains the Standish emblem of the owl and the rat, with the date 1793.

Wigan War Memorial was unveiled on the 17th October 1925, by General, the Hon. Herbert Alexander Lawrence, K.C.B.

The unveiled war memorial, 1925.

Wigan Parish Church showing the war memorial.

A row comprising dwelling houses, shops and warehouses, stood in Market Place, Standish, which completely hid St.Wilfrid's Church from view. The terrace was known as 'Spite Row' and it was contended that Roman Catholics built the properties about 1800 to spoil the approach to the church. This seems unlikely because, despite being Catholic, the Standish family held the advowson for Standish Church. (Advowson - Ecclesiastical law - the right of presentation to a vacant benefice).

It had long been considered that 'Spite Row' was a disfigurement. In 1880 Mr. Maskell Peace, then living at Ashfield House, Standish, who was Town Clerk of Wigan, proposed that the buildings should be removed and offered £500 towards the purchase. The scheme proved unsuccessful.

All the buildings in 'Spite Row' became vacant in October 1929 and J.M.Ainscough seized the opportunity to purchase them for demolition. He prevailed upon Sir Giles Gilbert Scott to prepare a plan for restoration of the site following demolition and with his assistance a London architect prepared a suitable design. The Corporation subsequently accepted the proposals.

'Spite Row' was finally demolished in November 1930 and the site was cleared and grassed over. The area was then fenced with a low stone wall. The appearance of the town's well was improved and the stocks were removed and replaced in their original position near to the ancient cross in Market Place. A long cherished dream had at last been fulfilled.

J.M.Ainscough died suddenly at his home in Parbold on the 8th January 1937, aged 82 years. Amongst the many tributes paid, it was said of him that he was "The kindest man. The best conditioned and unwearied spirit in doing courtesies". Mrs. Margaret Ainscough died on the 25th April 1946.

The old drinking well in Market Place, Standish, circa 1934. During the Second World War an American serviceman reversed an army truck into the well canopy causing damage, which necessitated its demolition. The well was also sealed. Only recently has the canopy been replaced.

The well is visible on this photograph, taken circa 1950, before the canopy was re-erected.

A Standish Landmark to Go.

9·11·29

Photo by—   J. Blackburn, 270, Wallgate.

"SPITE ROW."

An o'd landmark is on the point of disappearing from the oldest portion of the village of Standish, this being the block of ten houses in Market place, Standish, known locally as "Spite Row." As the above photograph shows, these houses to a great extent obscure the Parish Church immediately behind them, and the local legend has it that the houses were built by a Roman Catholic after the Reformation with the express object of hiding the church from public view, the church then, of course, having ceased to house the Catholics, and become the place of worship for the then new Church of England. In those days the Standish Parish Church had no spire, so that the object of the builder of the houses, if the legend be true, was more easily accomplished than it would have been to-day. The whole ten houses are now empty, the last having been vacated quite recently, and the families who had been living there have been absorbed in local Council houses, and in other houses which had become vacant. The property has been bought by a Wigan gentleman, who is a Protestant, on the condition that the Standish Urban District Council pull them down to disclose the Parish Church once more to uninterrupted view, and they are already in course of demolition, as the Council have decided to go on with a scheme of street improvement at that spot by widening the roadway.

The bronze plaque set into the stonework of the lamp reads, "Standish with Langtree Urban District Council. This plot of land, formerly the site of ten buildings, was dedicated to the public by James Martland Ainscough, Esquire, J.P., for the improvement of his native village. A.D. 1930".

Standish Market Place as it appeared after the demolition of 'Spite Row'.

STANDISH HALL

A detailed description of Standish Hall, as it existed in 1910, appears in the Victoria County History of Lancashire, volume 6, pages 196&7.

The hall was situated to the south west of the village on an eminence overlooking the valley of the River Douglas. When originally constructed in 1574, the residence was of the H design, comprising timber and plaster on a stone base.

Many alterations were carried out to the property. Towards the end of the 17th century the middle section of the original building formed only a part of the east wing. A number of the external walls had been rebuilt in brickwork and, to the north, a brick wing had been added. A chapel replaced the south wing in 1742-3.

A three storey, square, brick wing, built in 1748, formed the principal part of the house. In 1822 a long, single storey wing, was added which comprised dining and drawing rooms. All the roofs were covered with stone slates, and the half-timbered section had quatrefoil panels, with a long window, containing nineteen lights, above.

In 1910 the great hall, originally 36ft. by 17ft., was being used as a billiard room. Some oak panelling remained in the corridor and one of the bedrooms, other rooms had been modernised. There was a good staircase with turned balusters. A fireplace in one of the bedrooms bore a large plaster shield containing the Standish arms and crest, with cherubs.

Dimensions of the chapel were, chancel 13ft. 6ins. by 13ft., and nave 29ft. 8ins. by 19ft. 6ins. However, at this time the chapel was in a dilapidated condition, having been disused for a long period. It was brick built with gabled ends, with a wooden turret at the west and clock in the gable. The plaster of the ceilings and walls was broken and falling to pieces, and the sanctuary had been stripped of its ornamentation. The carved rails and classic altarpiece, with Tuscan columns and broken pediment, remained.

A moat once encircled the hall but this was filled in about 1780. Several of the spout heads at the property bore initials and dates, including one referring to Ralph and Mary Standish in 1748, and one relating to Charles Standish dated 1822.

Standish Hall, circa 1900.

Standish Hall, circa 1900.

View in Standish Hall gardens, circa 1900.

The old drawing room, Standish Hall, showing the ornate fireplace, circa 1910.

These illustrations of Standish Hall appear in the catalogue for the sale of the Standish Estate in 1921.

Beech Walk, Standish, circa 1910. The lodge to the right is Beech Lodge, which was the gatehouse for Standish estate.

Beech Walk Lodge, Standish, circa 1920.

Beech Walk, Standish, circa 1920.

Standish Hall, circa 1950.

EDUCATION IN STANDISH

Standish Free Grammar School for Boys

Mrs. Mary Langton of Hall o'th Hill, Heath Charnock, founded the Standish Free Grammar School for Boys in 1603. The school stood on land at the junction of Green Lane and School Lane, Standish.

Contained in a Charity Commissioner's report are details of an endowment of £64-4s-4d per annum, arising from the rents of lands, and the interest of £270, left by Mrs. Mary Smalley. Reverend William Leigh, the Rector of Standish, who succeeded Richard Moody on the 17th November 1586, further augmented the income for the grammar school in 1633, and there followed many other benefactions in favour of the school.

Richard Lathom was headmaster of the grammar school for 49 years. He died on the 3rd January 1817, aged 69 years.

A second master for the school was employed in 1863, at a salary of £25 per annum, together with lodgings in the schoolhouse, which was erected in 1796. Extensions were made to the school building in 1863, 1878 and 1897.

School fees were abolished on the 1st April 1904.

A total of 350 boys were attending the grammar school in 1908, which was the highest number ever recorded.

The school was managed by a board of governors, eight in total, the Rector of Standish Parish Church acted as chairman. In 1946 the headmaster was W. Garner, with T.Snape, M.A., as his assistant and four female teachers, Miss M.C.Light, Miss O. Holding, Mrs. M. Bradshaw and Mrs. H. Goodwin. Reverend W.S.Mellor, M.A., was clerk to the Trustees.

A school garden was provided in 1910 where the boys were taught the rudiments of horticulture.

Standish Grammar School for Boys was re-named, Standish C of E Boys' Primary School, in August 1951.

Eventually, the old grammar school merged with Standish Girls' School on Rectory Lane. Both schools continued to be run in conjunction with each other whilst new school premises were built on Rectory Lane.

Transfer to the new school was done in phases, as the various stages of the structure were completed. The two participating educational establishments were finally amalgamated at the new premises on the 7th January 1965.

The Bishop of Blackburn officially opened the school on the 3rd April 1965, and it was entitled, St. Wilfrid's Junior Mixed School.

Standish Grammar School was demolished in 1968 and the site is presently occupied by a care home for the elderly.

On this photograph of a class of boys at the grammar school are the headmaster, W. Garner (left), and Mr. T. Snape, a member of the teaching staff. The pupils who have been identified are, Back Row (left to right) I. Wilkinson, J. Critchley, ?, I. Lowton, J. Marrow, ?,?,?. Middle Row (l-r) A. Babb, ?, N. Bentham, ?, D. Dawson, J. Prescott, F. Collier, F. Osborne, J. Whitley. Front Row (l-r) ?, A. Andrews,?,?,?, D. Elsey, T. Hill, B. Andrews, ?, H. Heaton.

Teaching staff at Standish Grammar School, circa 1910.

Classroom at Standish Grammar School, circa 1915.

Boys working in the garden at the grammar school, circa 1915.

STANDISH GRAMMAR SCHOOL

Report for Term ending _July 1945._

Name _Alan Andrews_   Class _I_   Age _8_

No. in Class: **36**   Times Absent: 0

Position: **8th**   Times Late: 0

Subject.	Examination Mark		Remarks.
ENGLISH:			
Composition	45	(50)	A very good effort.
Language	38	(50)	Good.
Dictation	45	(50)	Very good.
Reading	35	(50)	Is making satisfactory progress.
~~Poetry~~ Spell	24	(50)	Will improve with reading.
Literature	10	(40)	
Writing	10	(10)	Can do some really good work.
ARITHMETIC:			
Mental	16	(20)	A very good effort.
Mechanical	25	(40)	Is sometimes careless in these two
Problems	31	(40)	subjects — no results above.
Geography	25	(50)	Very interested
History	38	(50)	Is keenly interested in this subject
Science or Nature Study	30	(50)	Also interested here.
Art	45	(50)	Does very good work.
Handicraft		(50)	
Practical Drawing		(50)	
Physical Training			
Music			
Scripture			

Class Teacher's Remarks: _Alan has made good progress. Tho' I think he could have made better — had he not been given to playfulness at lesson times._

Class Teacher _M. Bradshaw._

Head Master _WGarner_

Standish Grammar School, end of term report for Alan Andrews, July 1945.

Standish Grammar School football team, circa 1920.

Standish Grammar School, circa 1900.

The site of the old grammar school is presently occupied by 'Greenacres' care home for the elderly.

STANDISH GIRLS' SCHOOL

Standish Girls' School, in Rectory Lane, was originally built in 1829 as a Sunday school and was taken over for educational purposes by the National Schools Movement. The downstairs accommodation of the premises was used as an Infants' School. It also incorporated Miss Mary Smalley's School, originally founded in 1797.

The school was extended in the 1890's, the formal foundation stone laying ceremony being conducted on the 19th September 1891.

Cookery classes were introduced at the school in 1899, and the curriculum was gradually broadened to include local visits to railway stations, coal-mines, textile factories, etc.

On the 1st April 1906, the name of the school was changed to, Standish with Langtree Girls' and Infants' School.

Senior girls, aged 11 years and over, ceased to use the school with effect from the 19th December 1958. They were transferred to secondary schools in the district. However, the premises re-opened as a Junior Girls' School. Amalgamation with Standish C of E Boys' Primary School, took place until the transfer to the newly built St. Wilfrid's Junior Mixed School in 1965.

Class of infants at Standish Girls' and Infants' School, Rectory Lane, Standish, circa 1910.

Cookery class at the school during 1915.

Girls' class, circa 1920.

Standish Girls' and Infants' School was last used as St. Wilfrid's Church Club, and is presently undergoing refurbishment to be incorporated into a housing development.

Standish Girls' School, senior 1V class, with their headmistress, Miss Foy, photographed on the 16th April 1951.   Amongst the pupils are, back row (left to right), Elsie Goodier, Elsie Worthington, ?, Edna Jerstice, Enid Baxendale, ?, ?, Brenda Tidmarsh, Jean Martindale, ?, Miss Foy. Front row (l-r) Irene Melling, Barbara Wright, Barbara Simm, Jean Worthington, Margaret Haywood, Freda Smethurst, Enid Cowburn, Bernice Simpson and Doris Atherton.

St. Wilfrid's Schools, Rectory Lane, Standish, 2003.

St. Wilfrid's School, Rectory Lane, Standish. Mr. Ralph Bassett, the headmaster, and Mrs. Alice Carson are pictured with pupils amongst whom are John Robinson, Linda Whalley and Billy Ball.

Standish St. Marie's R C Primary School

Education for young people was often provided by private tuition or instruction from the Parish Priest. In 1865, however, a cottage in Almond Brook Road, Standish, situated opposite the Cat i'th' Window, was used as a school. After a period of only four years the demand for places had risen to the extent where an extension of the premises became necessary. Mrs. Frances Taylor of Strickland House, and Miss Cecilia Walmesley, officiated at the foundation stone laying ceremony for the extension in 1869.

Successive Parish Priests at St. Marie's R C. Church, always took a keen interest in securing education for the children of the parish. Father Corlett was the inspiration for the new school extension in 1869, and Father Barry worked diligently for the provision of a separate infants' school, which became a realisation when premises were constructed on the Cat i'th' Window site. Further extensions were made to the school premises in 1896 and 1898. The Sisters of Charity of St. Paul taught all school subjects from 1927 onwards, and they were accommodated at the old school house.

Her Majesty's Inspector for Schools visited St. Marie's School on the 16th and 17th March 1953. The report indicates that there were 216 boys and girls in attendance, with ages ranging from 41/2 years to 15 years. The children were arranged in six classes, and teaching staff comprised the headmistress, who was a nun, two assistant masters and four assistant mistresses. All the staff were suitably qualified to teach. Full-length screens were used to divide the various classrooms. School equipment and facilities were adequate.

In the early 1960's, mining subsidence began to affect the school building. A crack appeared in the playground caused by underlying subsidence, and it took nine tons of in-filling material to remedy. Evidence of further cracks appearing rendered the premises dangerous and resulted in an application being made to the Ministry of Education for the provision of a new school building.

An entirely new school was to be built on Avondale Street, Standish, commencing on the 25th January 1965.

The old school in Almond Brook Road was finally closed on the 6th April 1966. Transfer to the new school premises took place on the 21st April 1966, following the Easter break. The Auxiliary Bishop of Liverpool, the Right Reverend Augustine Harris, conducted the official opening ceremony for the new school on the 26th November 1966.

St. Marie's old school, convent and schoolhouse were subsequently demolished.

St. Marie's R.C. School,
Almond Brook Road,
Standish,
circa 1908.

Teaching staff at St. Marie's school, circa 1920. Miss Foster, the headmistress, is in the centre and the young boy to her left is her nephew, Bernard Foster. Mrs. McClarney, Miss Seagrave, Mrs. Cheetham, Miss Holden and Miss Hilton are also pictured.

Memoranda re St. Marie's School.

1850-1860. Francis Dowd, whose real name was Berry and who was the uncle of Dr. Berry of Wigan, kept a school for a few children at Scrap Cottage, off the road leading from Four Lane ends, Wrightington, to Lion's school. He was a cripple. He had once been a teacher in Ireland, and later as a stone mason he met with an accident. Thereafter he kept a school.

1850 Old Patsy Burns' father, (Tommy Runey) taught Catholic children their catechism at night in a house with a mud floor in Preston Road. The children took in turn a candle or a lump of coal. Coal then cost about 1d per cwt!

A room in what was later Sandy Pear's Farm was an early school (not C) Later a room near the 'Eagle, now the Black Bull, and then the Band Rm.

At the Hermitage for many years the Priest kept a night school where he gave children both religious and secular instruction

1865 Catholic Day School begun in the School House, which later became the convent.. opposite the Cat ith Window house.

1869 Main school built by Fr. Corlett

1879 Infants School built by Fr. Barry.

1896 New Senior Class Room. New Toilets and shelter.

1898 Extra Infants class room and two shelters

1929 Sisters of Charity of St. Paul were installed in the old School House and took charge of education in school.

1933 Water system introduced.

1935 Electric Light installed at a cost of £55.

Present Church

Foundation Stone blessed and laid by Bp. O'Reilly   24th June, 1883
Church solemnly opened by Bp. O'Reilly   18th May 1884
Church consecrated by Archbishop Keating   15th May 1924.

Residence of Priests

Up to 1825 at Standish Hall   1825-1828 "School House"   1828-1908 Hermitage
1908-   Presbytery.

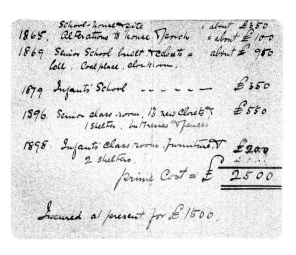

School-house site   : about £350
1865. Alterations to house } parish   : about £100
1869. Senior School built, toilets =   about £950
loll, Coalplace, cloakroom.
1879. Infants' School - - - - - - £350
1896. Senior class room, 16 new Closets } £550
1 shelter, buttresses & fences
1898. Infants' class rooms, furniture & } £200
2 shelters.
Prime Cost = £ 2500
Insured at present for £1500.

*Concert at St. Marie's Church Hall, circa 1915.
Agnes Fairhurst has been identified as first on the left
on the back row.*

*St. Marie's Boys Jazz Band, photographed in the
schoolyard, circa 1915.*

Children from St. Marie's school attending a church bazaar at the church hall in 1961. A game of Housey Housey or Bingo is in progress.

Doctor Malone cuts the first sod for the construction of St. Marie's new school in Avondale Street, Standish, on the 25th January 1965.

St. Marie's R.C. Primary School, Avondale Street, Standish, 2003.
The school building is presently undergoing extensive repairs.

THE LAST TRAM TO STANDISH

It was not without difficulty that the tramway from Wigan was extended from its terminus at Elmfield Road, via the Boar's Head, along Wigan Road to the centre of Standish.

The Wigan Corporation Act of 1901, passed on the 9th August 1901, authorised an extension of the existing tramway into Standish. However, Standish Urban District Council had insisted on imposing conditions before the extension went ahead, and these were incorporated into the legislation. In summary, the conditions amounted to several roads being widened including Boar's Head railway bridge, the gauge of the track to be consistent with that from Wigan to Elmfield Road, a workman's fare for the single journey, not to exceed one penny, and Standish U.D.C. was to have the option to purchase the line within its boundary after 14 years instead of the usual 21 years.

Tram services were very frequent. For example, in 1909 the timetable for April shows the following,

Monday to Friday
4-30am and every 15 minutes to 12noon
12-20pm and every 20 minutes to 8pm
8-15pm and every 15 minutes to 10-45pm
Saturday
As Monday to Friday until 12noon
12-10pm and every 10 minutes to 11-20pm
Sunday
1pm and every 15 minutes to 2pm
2-20pm and every 15 minutes to 10-20pm

Extra cars to Boar's Head
Monday to Friday
12-10pm and every 20 minutes to 7-50pm
Then 10-45pm
Saturday - 11-30pm
Sunday
2-10pm and every 20 minutes to 10-30pm.

Weather conditions sometimes caused disruption to the tram services, particularly in wintertime. For example, on Saturday, 11th January 1913, the weight of snow on overhead power lines in Standish brought down the overhead cable onto the tramway causing a stoppage lasting several hours.

In the winter of 1930/31, negotiations began to secure the abandonment of the tramway system and replace it with a bus service. Agreement with Standish U.D.C., once again proved difficult due to their insistence that the bus service should be no more frequent than the tram service. Despite protestations from Wigan that this would mean an inferior transport service because the buses had less passenger carrying capacity then trams, Standish won the day. The last tram to Standish ran on Saturday, 28th March 1931

Procession of witness in High Street, Standish, circa 1910. The tram tracks and overhead power lines can be seen on this old walking-day photograph.

Wigan Road, Standish, circa 1920. The tramway system is evident in this old view of the entrance to the village.

A Wigan Corporation tram outside the Boar's Head Inn, Standish, circa 1910.

Employees of Wigan Corporation Tramways, circa 1910.

High Street, Standish, at its junction with Church Street, showing the track bed for the tramways, circa 1920.

Terminus for the tramway system at Standish, circa 1920.

Double-decked tram in Park Road, Wigan, circa 1920.

COAL MINING IN STANDISH

When Standish Hall Estate was sold in March 1921, the following sentence appeared in the General Remarks section, concerning the sale. "The whole of the minerals are reserved from the sale".

Madame Standish, the widow of the last owner of the estate, Henry Noailles Widdrington Standish, therefore retained ownership of all the coal under estate lands and all the colliery sites. The Wigan Coal and Iron Company worked all the mines at this time and a considerable amount of rental was paid to Madame Standish for the privilege. Madame Standish died on the 12th October 1933, and ownership of the mineral rights at Standish passed to her niece, Mlle. M.M.A.E. de Montersquiou Fezenzac, who was married to Charles Marie Jean Widor.

An amalgamation involving the Wigan Coal and Iron Company, Pearson and Knowles, and a number of other companies; was made sometime after 1930. The newly formed concern was entitled the Wigan Coal Corporation. Rental dues were still paid to Madame Fezenzac Widor.

On the 1st July 1942, during the Second World War, the Government of the day took over all seams of coal, which they were empowered to work under legislation, the Coal Mines Act, 1938. Standish was included, and Madame Fezenzac Widor was compensated for the loss of the Standish Estate minerals and rental dues. A valuation assessed her loss at £100,148, which sum was duly paid.

The French connection with Standish ceased when, following the death of Madame Widor in the 1960's, the new owner, the Vicomte de Noailles, sold his manorial rights to a Wigan based company. In due course, the Opencast Executive of the National Coal Board, formed in 1947, acquired the Standish Estate.

In a paper entitled, "Transactions of Mining Engineers", volume 117, the following description appears of the Wigan Coalfield. "Few areas in this country were more richly provided with accessible coal seams, and few have been more extensively worked over the centuries". However, "The Wigan Coalfield is extensively faulted. The direction of the main faults is parallel to the Pennine Chain (that is N.N.W. - S.S.E. direction), and the resulting blocks of strata are again shattered by cross faulting.

With an abundance of coal to mine, it was essential to be able to transport the coal cheaply and conveniently to the available markets. Initially, a network of tramways was constructed to carry the coal to the River Douglas, which had been made navigable to the River Ribble, and was opened about 1742. The most important tramway in Standish ran from Robin Hill to Crooke. The arrival of the Leeds and Liverpool Canal in 1774 meant that the River Douglas fell into disuse.

Sometime after the completion of the Wigan branch of the Leeds and Liverpool Canal in 1777, a subterranean waterway was constructed connecting the Standish coal-mines directly with the canal. A condition of the lease granted to Standish Colliery Company by Charles Towneley and Edward Towneley Standish, on the 26th June 1798, was that an open cut or trench and a sough or tunnel, be made from the canal between Wigan and Liverpool to connect with the mines under Standish, during the first 25 years of the term of the lease.

Once the underground canal was built, it stayed in use for many years. Unfortunately, it was at too high a level to work the more important coal seams. However, it also served to drain water from the workings. The coal-carrying boats were propelled by men lying on their backs on the decking, and 'footing' or 'walking' along the walls of the tunnel. By 1845 the underground canal was obsolete, one of the main reasons being the development of the railway system.

Railways developed rapidly in the nineteenth century, and the invention of the steam locomotive soon resulted in a vast network of track being laid in south- west Lancashire.

An amusing story exists concerning the cast iron wheels of the old railway wagons used for transporting coal. The hubs and spokes were removed and the rims, which were about 30 inches in diameter, were sawn in half. The two halves of the rim were then used as 'fenders' in front of fireplaces in local pubs. The reason was that when fights broke out between the colliers, as they often did, the fender proved too heavy to lift for use as a weapon or to cause damage with.

In 1863, some 48 collieries were operating in the Wigan district, producing 4 million tons of coal per annum. When the coal-mines were Nationalised in 1947, only ten pits remained in the Wigan Coalfield proper, namely Alexandra, Chisnall Hall, Ellerbeck, Welch Whittle, John, Giant's, Victoria, Mains, Moss and Pemberton. Their combined annual output was 1,299,000 tons of coal, which necessitated the pumping of 4 tons of water for every ton of coal mined.

Electricity Generating Power Stations were the main customers for coal from Nationalisation in 1947. Other outlets included the domestic trade for household fires, cotton mills, paper mills, linoleum works, etc. A quantity was also supplied to the railways and a considerable tonnage was shipped by canal barge from Crooke to Liverpool.

A new coal washery was built near to the site of Gidlow Pits in 1947/1948, to replace an earlier plant situated near to John Pit. Standish Hall Drift Mine was opened in 1950, and Robin Hill Drift Mine in 1953. However, the optimism felt at this expansion proved to be a false dawn.

Gradually the coal - mines in the district reduced production and finally closed. There were a variety of causes for redundancy including exhaustion of stocks, unworkable seams and flooding. John Pit closed in April 1954. Victoria Colliery closed in 1958. Giant's Hall Colliery closed in January 1961.

Eventually, Robin Hill Drift Mine was the last working colliery in Standish, and this ceased production on the 29th November 1963, marking the end of an era.

Mining played an important part in shaping the character of individuals and gave families the security of a wage through some extremely difficult times. The occupation was dangerous and many lives were lost in the extraction of coal. There was also much suffering caused by industrial diseases associated with the work. In token remembrance of the era of coal mining in the Standish district, a small coal wagon, which doubles as a flower container, has been sited on land off High Street, opposite the police station.

Welch Whittle Colliery, situated in Coppull, was originally sunk about 1855, but closed in 1880. It was eventually re-opened by the Blainscough Colliery Company Ltd. Two new pits were sunk between 1892 and 1894. Closure took place in February 1960.

Hilton House and Red Moss Coal Company, first opened Ellerbeck Colliery about 1870, but the firm was only short lived and, in October 1877, the mine was purchased by the Hicbibi Coal and Cannel Co. Ltd. A succession of owners then followed until the late 1920's when the Adlington Coal Company Ltd., owned it. Ellerbeck Colliery was closed for a short period in 1932, when it was resumed under the ownership of the Blackrod Colliery Co. Ltd. Following the Nationalisation of the mining industry in 1947, the mine was finally closed in August 1965.

Advertisements for the Wigan Coal and Iron Company and Pearson and Knowles, who amalgamated with other colliery companies, sometime after 1930, to form the Wigan Coal Corporation.

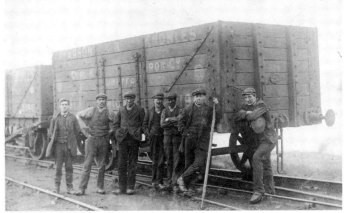

Pearson and Knowles coal wagon, circa 1910.

Advertisement included in the Wigan Coal and Iron Company's Almanac for 1896.

Langtree Colliery or Langtree Hall Colliery, was situated near to the junction of Preston Road and Pepper Lane, Standish. Originally sunk in 1857, the mine was worked until it was finally abandoned in March 1932.

The Prospect Pits were situated off Wigan Road, Standish, not far from Prospect House. Only two coal seams were worked at this colliery, the Wigan 4ft mine and the Wigan 5ft mine. Both Prospect Pits and the nearby Gidlow Pits, ceased to produce coal around 1910, but were retained for pumping purposes. Prospect Pits were eventually closed in September 1934.

old Elms Wigan Lane

In times of strike or undue hardship, coal was often retrieved from the spoil heaps and used to either supplement one's supply or for sale to help others. It was technically illegal and was known as coal picking. These two post card views show coal pickers at the Old Elms Pit, Wigan Lane, and Rookwood Pit. The latter is dated 28th March 1912.

John Pit Colliery with Taylor Pit visible in the background. The old engines were used for shunting coal on the mineral lines. 'Wantage' engine is to the right with 'Robin Hill' engine behind it, circa 1950.

THE WIGAN COAL CORPORATION LIMITED

The Directors request the pleasure of the company of

Mr A. Seddon

at the Opening of the PITHEAD BATHS

AT

JOHN COLLIERY,   AT 2-0 P.M.

AND

GIANTS HALL COLLIERY, AT 2-30 P.M.

- BY -

The Rt. Hon. The Earl of Crawford and Balcarres, K.T.

Monday, 27th June, 1938.

R.S.V.P. TO
J. RUTTER,
GIANTS HALL COLLIERY,
STANDISH,
NR. WIGAN

BUFFET

Invitation from the Wigan Coal Corporation to Mr. A. Seddon, to attend the official opening of the pithead baths at Giant's Hall Colliery, on the 27th June 1938.

WORKPEOPLE'S TRIP.—The workpeople employed at the Worthington Hall Collieries, near Standish, held their annual trip on Saturday. The favourite holiday resort of Blackpool had again been the place chosen by the men, and a small number of them journeyed from Wigan a few minutes after seven o'clock. At Standish and Coppull they were joined by large contingents of the workpeople, who mostly reside near the collieries, and then the train proceeded on its journey. Blackpool was reached a few minutes to nine, and the excursionists separated to visit the numerous places of amusement, the Winter Gardens, Raikes Hall, the Aquarium, and other places, to which they were admitted at a reduced price, being largely patronised by the trippers. In the evening most of the excursionists flocked to Raikes Hall, some to participate in the "latest novelties," bowling, &c., and others to spend a happy hour or two on the light fantastic toe. At dusk the visitors and those present in the beautiful grounds congregated together to witness the fireworks and the representation of the battle of Abu Klea, after which they left to catch their train, which left Blackpool about eleven o'clock and reached its destination at nearly one o'clock on Sunday morning.

Extract from the Wigan Examiner newspaper, dated the 24th July 1886, relating to the annual miners' outing to Blackpool.

Post card published by Starr's C.B.B. Series, Wigan, showing coal miners working a coal seam. The date 15/12/97 can be seen on the roof support.

Wigan Pit Brow Lassie, circa 1920.

Colliery girls at work, Douglas Bank Colliery, circa 1915.

Comic post card from the Will Smith's series, Wigan, 1906.

Crooke Coal Tippler, circa 1939. Woodcock Row is to the left with Van Outram's bread van making a delivery. Amongst the people gathered are Tom and Jackie Darwen (Darren) and Joe Booth.

Coal tub, sited off High Street, Standish, which commemorates the importance of coal mining in the district, 2003.

THE LEEDS AND LIVERPOOL CANAL

An Act of Parliament, passed on the 19th May 1770, authorised the construction of the Leeds and Liverpool Canal. The first sod was cut at Halsall, in West Lancashire, during 1770.

Open boats or barges, capable of carrying up to 20 tons, had used the Douglas Navigation from its completion in mid 1742. There was opposition to the proposed Leeds and Liverpool Canal for a number of reasons, one of the objectors being the Douglas Navigation Company who were afraid that their water supply would be prejudicially affected. In the event, the chief shareholders of the Douglas Navigation, Alexander Leigh and his son, Holt Leigh, sold the majority of their company shares to Jonathan Blundell and William Earle of Liverpool, who held them in trust for the Leeds and Liverpool Canal Company.

A branch canal was constructed to link the Leeds and Liverpool with the Douglas Navigation. It was 12 yards wide and 5'6" deep.

In 1774, the Leeds and Liverpool Canal was opened from Liverpool to Gathurst, and then via the Upper Douglas Navigation to Wigan.

It was not until 1816 that the Leeds and Liverpool Canal was finally completed and opened throughout.

The canal and the River Douglas run relatively close to each other, on the outskirts of Standish. The River Douglas is culverted near to Standish Bleachworks and then flows through Red Rock, and follows roughly the line of Chorley Road and Wigan Lane into the centre of Wigan. Looping its way through Haigh Plantations, the canal then flows parallel with Poolstock Lane into Ince. The two waterways again converge to the south west of Wigan town centre and follow a route, running almost in tandem, through Crooke and Gathurst, to Parbold.

There has been an upsurge in the use of canals for pleasure purposes in recent times, and the Leeds and Liverpool presently carries a great deal of craft.

This stone cottage stands close to the Leeds and Liverpool Canal at Red Rock.
A capstan can be seen in front of the property, circa 1900.

Canal bank at Gathurst, showing a horse-drawn barge, circa 1920.

The Navigation Inn, by the side of the Leeds and Liverpool Canal at Gathurst, circa 1910.

This interesting view shows both the Leeds and Liverpool Canal and the River Douglas, circa 1920.

RAILWAYS THROUGH STANDISH

Standish was once criss-crossed by a complicated railway network, with the main rail routes being connected to numerous mineral lines, which serviced the local collieries and factories. Standish railway station has long since closed, and it is now difficult to envisage the amount of permanent way track which once traversed the area. The only clues left to help identify much of the old railway system are the abandoned track-beds, which are difficult to properly locate. Nostalgia still lingers for the days of steam driven locomotives, when train services seemed more reliable, and travel relatively cheap. Despite the clean and efficient diesel driven locomotives of the present day, there remains a deep affection for the old steam driven workhorses of yesteryear, which with the passage of time have become imbued with a magical quality.

Rectory Lane, Standish, with Standish Railway Station, visible in the centre of the photograph, circa 1920.

0-6-0 Steam engine, number 52341, pulling coal wagons through Standish, circa 1950.

2-6-0 Steam engine, number 42894, travelling through Standish, on the 18th March 1953.

Standish Railway Station, circa 1945.

Gathurst Railway Station, circa 1949.

Diesel locomotive, number D447, climbing towards the Boar's Head.

STANDISH INDUSTRIES

Coal mining was once the chief industry of the district but many other concerns provided employment for the local populous, including cotton spinning and manufacture, bleaching, paper making, brick and tile works and brewing.

Whilst it is outside the scope of this work to provide detailed information of all the industrial concerns operating in the Standish district, a number of them are included.

Bradley Manufacturing Company Ltd., Bradley Lane, Standish, circa 1900. The rear of this post card contains the following information, Capital £50,000 in 50,000 shares of £1 each. Directors, Mr. James Bentham, Chairman, Rev. C.W.N.Hutton, Vice-Chairman, Mr. R. Gregory, Mr. Stephen Bentham, Secretary and Manager, Mr. G.R.Stott. LOANS received daily, small or large sums, Interest 41/2 per cent, free of Income Tax. Withdrawal at call.

Standish Works, Worthington, circa 1900. Standish bleach works, on the left of this photograph, was formerly a paper mill, which ceased trading in 1883. The following year, T. Taylor & Co. Ltd, commenced bleaching operations. In 1899 the Bradford Dyers' Association Ltd, took over the concern, and for a period introduced cloth dyeing but this was discontinued in 1907. The Standish bleach works used the Mayflower ship as their trademark, an allusion to Captain Myles Standish.

Standish bleach works is presently used as an industrial complex, comprising several operations. Whilst some parts of the works are well maintained, there is some dereliction about the place. These photographs, taken in 2003, show the works present day.

The old Standish bleach-works from Red Rock.

View across the complex from the Worthington side.

The lake in the work's grounds.

Mayflower Cottages, circa 1900. These attractive properties still overlook the works.

Lakeside Cottages, 2003.

Obverse and reverse of a bronze medal presented to members of the Fire Brigade at Standish bleach works on completing ten years service.

LOT 126.

(Coloured Yellow on Plan).

That Very Valuable Freehold Property

BEING PART OF

Standish Bleach & Dye Works

Situate in the Parish of Worthington on the Wigan to Chorley Road, 3 miles from the centre of Wigan and about ¼-mile from Standish L. & N.W.R. Station.

This Property consists of a portion of the extremely well built Bleach and Dye Works equipped to meet all modern requirements, with excellent water facilities and up-to-date equipments.

THE TOTAL AREA CONSISTS OF

3a. 3r. 14p. more or less,

which is practically all covered with buildings,

AS PER

SCHEDULE

Ordnance Enclosure.	Acreage.
44	3.584
3A	.072
44A	.020
2	.096
3	.070
	3.842

This lot is in the occupation of the Bradford Dyers Association.

OUTGOINGS.—Tithe Rent Charge (apportioned sum) 15s. 9d.

Obverse and reverse of a silver medal presented after twenty years service.

Entry from the catalogue for the sale of Standish estate in 1921, relating to Standish Bleach & Dye Works.

150

Mill Dam Cottage, circa 1900. The mill was operated on behalf of Standish Hall estate.

Another view of Mill Dam Cottage, similar in date, circa 1900, which was sold as part of the Will Smith's series of Wigan post cards.

The waterwheel of the mill was powered by Mill Brook. A dam erected behind the mill ensured a good head of water.

AND DISTRICT ADVERTISER, SATURDAY. JULY 23

300 Ton Chimney Felled at Gathurst

Photo by   J. Blackburn, Darlington-street East.

PASSING OF FAMILIAR LANDMARK.

The felling of the huge chimney near the railway at the Roburite and Ammonal Works, Gathurst, for many years a landmark in that particular part of the Wigan district, provided a great thrill for a large number of spectators at noon on Thursday. The chimney fell with a reverbrating crash, and a cloud of dust rose and drifted over the scene, but the job was only done after a very hard fight. The old chimney, in fact, died hard, and Mr. Harry Dickinson, of Newtown, the steeplejack, who brought it down, said afterwards that it was one of the stiffest jobs in his experience. The first blow at the chimney was struck about seven o'clock on Wednesday morning, but the sun had climbed across the heavens and sunk into the west on Wednesday evening, and the chimney still defied its tormentors. Shortly after eight o'clock Mr. Dickinson, who had anticipated having the chimney down by 2 p.m. that day gave up the job, and the tall stack was reprieved for a night.

Work was again resumed at eight o'clock the following morning, but it was not until 12.45 the afternoon that the chimney suddenly shivered and toppled over. The end came suddenly, and the steeplejacks had to run for it at the finish.

The chimney was fully 150 feet high, and it contained some 100,000 bricks, weighing in all about 300 tons. It was felled by the expedient knocking the bricks out of the base, but so well built was it that it stood defiant for nearly a day and a half before toppling over.

The picture shows the chimney, which was built about fifty years ago, and was one of the tallest stacks in the Wigan district, in its last moments. It had recently been bought by Mr. J. Berry, contractor, of Lathom and Southport, and the bricks will be used for building purposes.

Newspaper cutting, dated 23rd July 1932, relating to the demolition of the chimney at Roburite Works.

THE WHEELS OF COMMERCE

Trade Directories for the Standish district are included at Appendix 2, showing details for 1866 and 1923. The number and diversity of entries, means that it is not a practical proposition to include them all but a random selection does however, give the overall impression of those days when we were known as a "Nation of shopkeepers".

William Abbott's hardware shop, 41 Preston Road, Standish, circa 1900.

WM. ABBOTT,

41, Preston Road, Standish.

Dealer in LAMPS and LAMP OILS of all kinds.

MACHINERY OILS a Speciality.

RUGS, CARPETS, and MATS always in Stock.
ASH PANS, KETTLES, PANS, TOP BARS, FENDERS,
and all kinds of Enamel Ware.

COLLIERS' TOOLS, WRINGING MACHINES, &c., TO ORDER.

Baron's Standish Boot Stores, Preston Road, Standish, circa 1900.

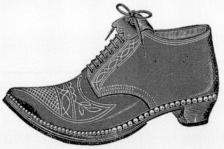
154

Whitehall, Standish, which occupied the site where Standish Library now stands, circa 1940.

On the back of the wagonette is the name Wm. Farrimond, Standish, circa 1920.

The Palace Cinema, High Street, Standish, circa 1930.

Standish Co-operative Society store is visible on the left of this walking day photograph with O.G.Rushton's store on the right.

Local advertisements, dating from the early 1900's.

ESTABLISHED 40 YEARS.

Howard and Son,

BUTCHERS, &c.,

36, High Street, Standish.

The Noted Shop for

**ENGLISH BEEF,
PORK, MUTTON,
LAMB, & VEAL.**

KILLED ON THE PREMISES FROM THE BEST MARKETS ONLY.

Specialities : HOME-MADE SAUSAGE, BRAWN, and PUDDINGS.

Home-Cured Hams and Bacon always in stock.

ORDERS CALLED FOR. OR BY POST, RECEIVE OUR BEST ATTENTION.

Joe Fairhurst, Beef & Pork Butcher.

IF you want some good home-killed Beef, Mutton, Lamb, Veal, or Pork, at a Reasonable Price, just give me a trial order. I will endeavour to please you . . . .

SPECIALITIES :

Pickled Tongues . .

Pickled Beef . . . .

Home-Cured Hams

. . . . . and Bacon

Rabbits . . . .

And one very

essential thing :

Cleanliness !

All Meat guaranteed English, Country Fed, and of the Best Quality . . . . . Orders punctually attended to.

Note the Address : 42, PRESTON ROAD, STANDISH.

157

Tom Wilding outside his cycle shop at 63 High Street, Standish, circa 1920.

Tom Wilding, with his two daughters, outside his garage on High Street, Standish, circa 1920.

Newsagents shop, Shevington Moor, circa 1950.

Gathurst Café, circa 1930.

AGRICULTURE

In the Mannex Directory for 1866, there are 44 farmers listed in Standish alone, Worthington had a further 9 farmers, Shevington had 24 farmers, Charnock Richard 24 farmers, and Welch Whittle 15 farmers. Therefore much of the land was given over to agriculture. In 1923, some 57 years later, farmers are no longer listed separately but included amongst the commercial sections of the respective district. Kelly's Directory for 1923 lists only 22 farmers in Standish, although Worthington had 10 farmers. Shevington also shows a reduction with 16 farmers indexed. Charnock Richard, however, shows an increase in the number of farmers with 38 farmers appearing, along with a number of small holders and poultry breeders. Welch Whittle records some 9 farmers.

Much of the farmland in Standish belonged to the Standish family and was sold when the estate was auctioned in 1921. A plan of the estate is included at the rear of this book, which identifies the land included in the sale.

Evan House Farm, Standish Lower Grounds, circa 1920. The farm was included in Standish Estate.

Ebenezer Peers Farm, Larkhill, off Rectory Lane, Standish, circa 1900. At this time the farm building was used as an Isolation Hospital for persons suffering from such diseases as smallpox, tuberculosis and scarlet fever.

Standish Hall Farm, 2003.

The interesting brickwork of these old building can be seen on this structure, along with the circular stone window frame.

Date stone built into the wall, relating to the Standish family and dated 1684.

Standish Hall Farm from the rear.

Worthington Hall Farm is an ancient hall connected with the Worthington family.

The outbuilding of Worthington Hall Farm are also indicative of great age.

Rectory Farm, Rectory Lane, Standish. This farm was once belonged to the church and supported the Rectory, which was situated on the opposite side of the lane. At the time that this photograph was taken the property was for sale. It has since been sold and substantially re-furbished.

Harvesting at Wrightington Hall, Wrightington, circa 1900.

THE SALE OF STANDISH ESTATE

The Standish family, and their estate, feature largely in the history of Standish. It is in many ways fortunate that the family papers, which date back generations, have been preserved locally. This has been due mainly to the generosity of the family and the foresight of a number of individuals who were astute enough to realise their importance in the long term.

On the death of the last surviving member of the Standish family, the estate was put up for auction. E.H.Tipping, Auctioneers, of 30 Cornmarket Street, Oxford, handled the sale which was held at the Empress Hall, Wigan, on Thursday and Friday, the 17th and 18th March 1921. The sales catalogue describes the Standish estate as follows. "This attractive freehold estate comprises an area of approximately 3,000 acres, including many accommodation farms and very excellent agricultural holdings (a large area with vacant possession) several fine residences, good dwelling houses and building plots, and woodlands.

A further sale was subsequently held to dispose of the houses and cottages around the village of Standish, which formed part of the estate.

Eighty lots went under the hammer on the first day, including Prospect House, residence and land; agricultural holding, 'Old Hall, Langtree'; garden and paddock, 'The Beeches', School Lane; Jane Standish Farm; Frodsham House Farm; Brockhurst Farm and Brimelow Farm.

On the second day of the sale a further fifty lots were offered, including Limes Farm, Standish; Giant's Hall Farm; Evan House Farm; Roburite Explosive Works; Cat i'th'Window Farm; Standish Hall; Standish Hall Farm; Manor House, Worthington; and Standish Bleach and Dye Works.

The two-day sale raised a total of £55,000 but the hall was withdrawn because only £4,800 was offered, which was considered far too low. The auctioneer informed those at the sale that an offer of £3,000 had been bid by an American for the oak panelling alone.

There are several versions of what happened to Standish Hall following the sale. One account, which is contained in the excellent book on Standish Collieries, states that the half-timbered middle portion of the hall, and the fine oak panelling, were sold to an American buyer, and subsequently shipped to the United States and rebuilt. Reverend Porteus comments that, "After the sale of the estate, the hall was dismantled, the oak fireplaces (which came originally from Borwick Hall), together with much panelling, were removed and sold". Messrs. Roberson of Knightsbridge, were the purchasers, and the source of this information was the Daily Mail of the 16th February 1922.

The text continues, "The hall is now (1923) being partly demolished in order to construct two separate residences", (by the purchaser, Mr. H. Baxter).

"The black and white building is entirely removed, also the chapel to the right of it. The uppermost storey has been taken away from the three-storied portion, and this part, now two-storied, made into a separate house. The extreme east end has been left standing to make another smaller house, part of the central building being removed to effect a separation between the two residences. In the removed portion here, which had probably been rebuilt in the 18th century, two huge timber frames were found, one at either end, completely concealed by brickwork. These evidently were gables of a timber house, and also indicate that there was a large hall or room with an open roof unceiled, the beams of which were moulded".

Wigan Public Library received donations of a clock gong or bell, from the domestic chapel, with the inscription R.S. 1743, 18 inches in diameter and bearing the name and mark of Luke Ashton, bell founder of Wigan, along with a smaller bell bearing the sign of a hunter's horn.

Standish Hall was used to billet troops during the Second World War, 1939-1945.

During 1980 the two properties built on the site of Standish Hall following its partial demolition were also demolished. Nothing now remains of this once fine old building. Trees are growing on the site and, apart from the odd pieces of stonework and two brick built structures, the area has returned to nature.

Entry from the catalogue for the sale of Standish Estate in 1921, relating to Standish Hall.

LOT 116.
(Coloured Yellow on Plan).

WITH POSSESSION ON COMPLETION.

An Extremely Pleasantly Situated and Well Built

Country Mansion

of the Queen Anne type

KNOWN AS

Standish Hall

CONTAINING

20a. 3r. 10p. more or less.

SCHEDULE

Ordnance Enclosure.	Acreage.
409	10.785
408	6.910
418 part	3.117
	20.812

THE HOUSE, situate in its own well timbered grounds, contains :—

VESTIBULE and OUTER HALL 45-ft. by 7-ft. 6-ins.), Inner Hall, and a fine lofty suite of Reception Rooms, comprising—

DRAWING ROOM (31-ft. by 22-ft. 6-ins., with south aspect), containing fine Mahogany Doors with Ornamental Mouldings and Capitals.

DINING ROOM (35-ft. 9-ins. by 23-ft. 6-ins.), with fine Marble Mantelpiece.

MORNING ROOM or second Dining Room (19-ft. 6-ins. by 16-ft. 6-ins), with fine Carved Oak Chimneypiece and Overmantel, choice Old Oak Panelling and fine Moulded Ceiling.

STUDY (20-ft. by 11-ft.) with fine Carved Oak Chimneypiece and Overmantel.

NOBLE BILLIARD ROOM (29-ft. by 23-ft.), with windows opening to Lawn.

LAVATORY and CLOAK ROOM.

THE OFFICES comprise Butler's Pantry, House-keeper's Room, large well lighted Kitchen with Eagle Range, Scullery, and very ample other domestic offices.

ON THE FIRST FLOOR there are two Oak Panelled Bedrooms (21-ft. 6-ins. by 22-ft. and 16-ft. by 18-ft., respectively), Old Oak Room with Closet (14-ft. 6-ins. by 20-ft.), Black Oak Panelled Lounge with heavy beams forming the most ancient portion of the Hall (19-ft. by 14-ft.), in addition to which the bedroom accommodation comprises 14 Bed and Dressing Rooms, mostly of large size.

There are 3 excellent Bath Rooms, W.C's., etc.

THE CELLARAGE is capacious and suitable for all requirements.

Part of the Hall consists of a fine specimen of Early English half timbered work, in which are very fine Flemish and Early English Oak Panelling and Carving in a remarkably good condition and well worth the attention of connoisseurs. Adjoining is a disused Roman Catholic Chapel.

Outside are excellent Balliff's House (now 2 cottages), extensive Flower Gardens, Lawns and pleasant walks.

THE KITCHEN GARDENS are extensive, containing a fine brick wall, 4 large Vineries, one 24-ft. and three 28-ft. long.

A range of Green Houses, 3 fine Peach Houses, each 38-ft. long and 12-ft. wide.

THE PROPERTY is eminently suitable for a Religious Institution, Home or Hospital, affording very ample accommodation.

OUTGOINGS.—Tithe Rent Charge (apportioned sum) £1 10s. 5d.

N.B.—This House and the old residence which for centuries occupied the same site, the only remaining portion of which is the Early English Structure above referred to, was for a very lengthy period the home of the famous Standish Family.

The entrance to Standish Hall, showing the remains of a stone- wall, 2003.

The brick structure is all that remains on the site of Standish Hall, and appears to have been a greenhouse, 2003.

Adjacent to the pathway, which ran down the side of Standish Hall, is this structure, which is obviously of some age because it is built from hand-made bricks. Apparently, it was used as the ash-pit for Standish Hall, 2003.

A bungalow exists near to where Standish Hall once stood, and these two houses are situated some little distance away, 2003.

167

I was most interested to discover that the area around Standish Hall was used to billet troops during the Second World War (1939-1945). This interesting series of photographs was taken about 1940 and shows a number of the soldiers.

THE BREWER'S ART

Standish, in common with many other industrial areas in the north west of England was well served with licensed premises, and had it own brewery in School Street, Standish, operated by J.B. Almond.

Other breweries, besides J.B.Almond, supplied the public houses in Standish. These included Whittle Springs Brewery from Chorley, whose name appears above the Globe Inn, on an old photograph.

Several beer houses are listed in the 1866 Mannex Directory. These were generally small operations, often selling their own brewed ales. Some of the more conventional pubs in the Standish district date back centuries.

A number of interesting photographs of licensed premises are included along with information concerning them.

J.B.Almond's brewery wagon laden for delivery, circa 1920.

School Lane, Standish, circa 1920. The three-storey brewery building is visible to the right of centre.

Four views of Standish Brewery, School Lane, Standish, taken shortly before demolition in the 1980's.

The Boar's Head Hotel, Wigan Road, Standish, circa 1900.

A similar view of the hotel taken about the same date, 1900.

The harsh winter of 1940 is still remembered and this interesting shot of the Boar's Head, taken at that time, gives some idea of the difficulties caused by severe weather conditions.

The old and the new Seven Stars can be seen on the left and right of this photograph, respectively. 2003.

Close up view of the New Seven Stars.

The building on the right was once the Eagle and Child public house. The Lych Gate pub is on the left, 2003.

NEW SEVEN STARS HOTEL

Lounge Bar

Snacks   Music

Weddings & Parties catered for

Large Car Park

PRESTON ROAD

STANDISH   Tel. 2356

Proprietors: Mr. & Mrs. WILSON

An ALMOND house

Advertisement for the New Seven Stars, referring to J.B.Almond's Brewery.

The Black Horse pub, which stood on the corner of Almond Brook Road and Arbour Lane, Standish, circa 1910.

The Wheatsheaf Hotel, Preston Road, Standish, circa 1900.

Close-up views of the Wheatsheaf Hotel, circa 1960.

Standish Conservative Club, circa 1920.

Game of bowls in progress on Standish Conservative Club bowling green, circa 1920.

STANDISH CRICKET CLUB

Reverend Charles William Newton Hutton, Rector of St. Wilfrid's Church, Standish, between 1886 and 1938, initiated the purchase of land in Standish for the purpose of cricket and tennis. Rev. Hutton was the President of Standish Cricket Club from 1894 until the mid 1930's. The founding date for the club is not properly known but its centenary was celebrated in 1977.

In 1895, Standish C.C., applied to join the Wigan and District League. A groundsman was employed in 1898, at a salary of 3/3d per week. The first team professional and club groundsman was M.H.Watson, appointed in 1901, at a weekly fee of 25 shillings.

Standish C.C. won the Wigan League Championships in 1914. There was a cessation of activities during the First World War, with games resuming following the Armistice. In 1920 the team joined the West Lancashire Cricket League, winning the prestigious Salter Trophy that year. In the same year, two pavilions, a roller and a mower, were obtained from Haigh Parish Council Cricket Club for £16.

The club was in a position to buy its present ground outright in 1922, and continued to prosper, winning league championships in 1928 and 1929.

On the formation of the West Lancashire Cricket Association, in 1963, Standish C.C. became a member. The club subsequently enjoyed success, winning the Rathbone Trophy on three occasions, 1973, 1979 and 1981. They also won the John Heaton Memorial Trophy in 1973.

The Bolton and District Cricket Association, inaugurated on the 9th November 1888, admitted Standish C.C. to membership in 1984, since when further success has been achieved.

Standish Cricket Club, showing the pavilion, 2003.

Standish cricket field, with the water tower on the right, 2003.

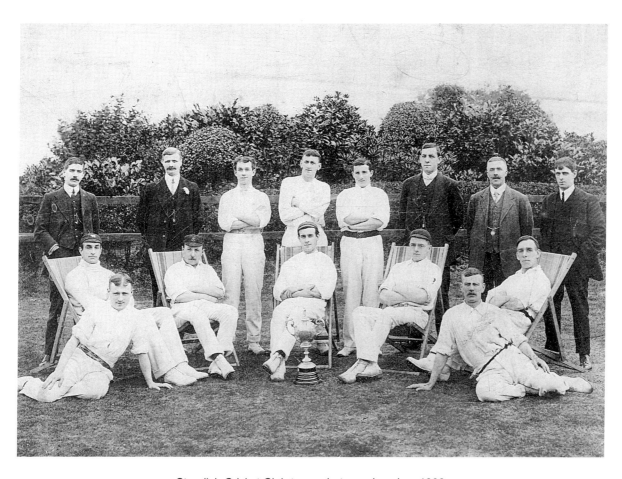

Standish Cricket Club team photographs, circa 1900.

STANDISH SPORTS AND PASTIMES

Without a section covering general sporting activities and pastimes, the overall impression of the town of Standish is incomplete. The game of cricket has already received mention in connection with Standish Cricket Club, and most of the schools were involved in football. Football was always an important competitor sport, more so than rugby, which has long enjoyed an avid following in nearby Wigan. Tennis and crown green bowling, were also enjoyed along with a myriad of other pastimes. Many of the townspeople, particularly the miners, were keen pigeon fanciers, and this sport still attracts good local support. Angling is also practised widely in this area, the canals and local reservoirs providing excellent venues. Where any sport is followed, there are invariably organised competitions, which attract the more proficient and offer the opportunity to compete for prestigious prizes.

Standish St. Wilfrid's Church Institute and Youth Club football team, circa 1954. The team manager was Peter Sedgewick and amongst the players are, (back row), Gordon Helm, Bill Green, Eric Cockram, Terance Hill, (front row), Bill Greenwood, Bill Mason, Terry Cliff, Tom Meehan and Alan Andrews.

St Marie's football team, 1910.
Back Row (left to right) Teddy Fairhurst, Tom Regan, Joe Carney, Martin Durkin, and Joe Corrigan.
Middle Row (l-r) Andy Fairhurst, Joe Stanton, and Joe Foster.
Front Row (l-r) Joe McLaren, William Abbott, Mike Regan (killed in action in the 1914-1918 war), George Fairhurst and Steve Whelan.

St. Marie's football team, circa 1930.

Standish Grammar School football team, circa 1960.
Mr. Jones is pictured with the team, which includes B. Ball, B. Taylor, J. Latimer, R. Unsworth, E. Birchall, B. Green, R. Hart, E.Walsh, D. Davis, B. Whalley, G. Hilton and G. Mason.

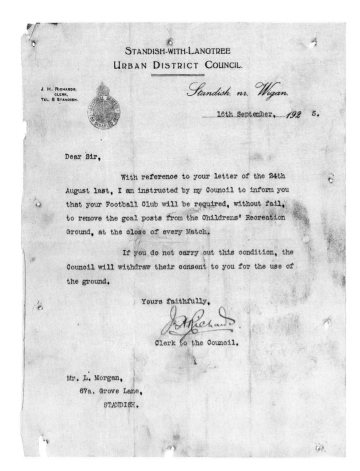

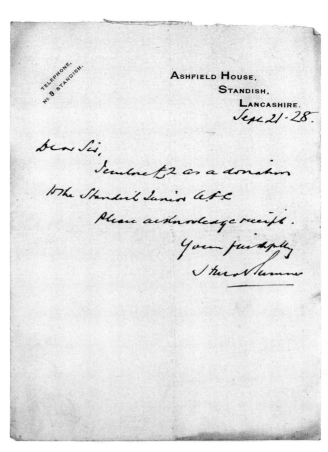

Copy of correspondence, dated 16th September 1925, between Standish Council and Leonard Morgan, who was secretary for the Standish junior football league.

Letter from Mr. Sumner of Ashfield House, Standish, dated 21st September 1928, offering a £2 donation towards the Standish Junior A.F.C.

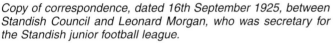

Correspondence relating to a disciplinary hearing against a member of Standish Grammar School, Sunday school football club, 1926.

250,000 MILES ON BICYCLE

DAILY DISPATCH 9.1-35.

Veteran Launches 'Over 50' Club

From a Special Correspondent

Wigan, Tuesday.

TO-NIGHT I met a man here who almost lives on wheels and who in his lifetime has cycled more than a quarter of a million miles.

He is Mr. Tom Hughes, the miner-cyclist of Wigan. He has cycled as a pastime for two-thirds of his 68 years.

For more than half a century—he started work when he was 11—until he retired from the Garswood Hall Collieries three years ago, Mr. Hughes had never been a day out of work in the pits.

His first machine, now nearly as old as himself and still preserved as a memento of the old days, was a "penny farthing."

He has cycled at home and abroad, and in the last seven years alone has exceeded 83,000 miles. Last year he covered 10,000 miles in this country and never boarded a train, tram, or bus.

Now he has formed the Autumn Tints Cycling Club, a .... club restricted to members over 50 years of age who are bald or grey.

OVER THE ALPS

Their next gathering will be on Sunday next at Appleton, near Warrington. The total ages of those expected to be present will exceed 1,500 years.

Mr. Hughes is captain of this novel club. The oldest member is Mr. H. R. Godwin, a Manchester business man in his 80th year, who always attends the cycling meets accompanied by his wife.

"Cycling has always kept me fit," Mr. Hughes told me.

"I have often cycled abroad, including a visit to the Passion Play at Oberammergau.

"Last year I had a cycling trip to France, Italy, and Switzerland with a Master of Arts and a Foreign Office official for companions. I then cycled over the Alps, and one night slept 4,500 feet up."

A son of Mr. Hughes has established more than one wheeling record.

Mr. Hughes has 22 grandchildren, and he believes they will all live to a ripe age if they take to the wheel and the open road like he himself has done.

HOW WE ROD IN 87.

Mr. Tom Hughes on his penny-farthing bicycle.

Cycling was a very popular pastime in the 1920's and 1930's with one of its more famous exponents, Tom Hughes, resident in nearby Wigan. Tom Wilding's shop in High Street, Standish, catered for local needs.

Tom Hughes and family, 1938

The Independent Order of Oddfellows still has a strong following in Standish, and this post card view of lodge members, taken about 1910, gives an impression of the membership.

Oddfellows' Hall, Church Street, Standish, 2003.

Standish Girls' Friendly Society, Nativity play, circa 1938.
Back Row (commencing from the left) L. Norris, M. Whiteside, Ida Hyatt, C. Goodwin, Louise Collier, Olive Ryding, M. Smith, B. Cowburn, P. Tickle, D. Roper, M. Banks, M. Hill, A. Whiteside, B. Barlow, A. Barlow, G. Tranter, M. Ryding, M. Hodge, J. Ellison, D. West.
Front Row (l-r) M. Johnson, M. Dawber, M. Cooper, M. Hodge, M. Howarth (as Mary holding the baby Jesus), A. Ecclestone, A. Valentine, Elsie Keogh.

The 26th Wigan St. Wilfrid's Brownie Pack, Standish, was the first to be formed in the town, about 1940.
Back Row (from left to right) D. Mills, M. Ryder, B. Cowburn, M. Bankes, A. Hilton, M. Ryding, A. Hewitt, ?, A. Ryding, B. Mills.
Middle Row (l-r) J. Preston, M. Meaking, B. Mason, F. Rainford, B. Justice, S. Livesey, J. Davies, J. Rainford.
Front Row (l-r) J. Dawber, G. Hurst, B. Anderson, B. Willis, J. Stringfellow, C. Roby.

Standish Girl Guides outside St. Wilfrid's church, 1950. The Guide Leader is Olwyn Wilding and amongst those identified are, B.R.Bronwyn Wilding, Enid Baxendale, Margaret Haywood, Enid Cowburn, and Elsie Worthington.

Standish Bandeaux Morris Dancers on J.B. Almond's field taking part in a competition on the 16th May 1953. Standish Parish Church spire can be seen to the left with almond's Brewery chimney nearby.

Standish Girls' Training Corps photographed in Standish Methodist Church in 1951, during a musical item. Those identified are, Jean Peet, Doreen Jones, Brenda Tidmarsh, Enid Baxendale, Esther Langton, Elsie Turner, Enid Cowburn, and Freda Smethurst.

HIGH DAYS AND HOLIDAYS

There are numerous societies and organisations, which cater for leisure pursuits, and it was not beyond the capabilities of individuals to create their own amusements. People who work hard generally tend to play hard, and there is little doubt that Standish people knew how to have a laugh and enjoy themselves, as well as providing entertainment for others. The photographs included below capture precious moments when life became less serious.

Standish ladies ready for a day out, circa 1920.
Third from the right on the back row is Jane Urmston.

Outing from Standish church to Windermere, circa 1926.
Cyril Birchall is the small boy on the left.

Outing to Southport for the children of members of the Standish British Legion, circa 1935.
Amongst the children enjoying themselves on the Peter Pan playground at Southport are,
A. Cooper, M. Ryding,
D. Ryding, G. Tranter,
J. Makinson, M. Gray,
H. Andrews, E. Gray,
B. Cowburn, B. Wilson,
J. Davies, N. Baxendale,
N. Ryder, M. White,
J. Rawlinson, D. Roper, and
E. Keogh.

The four men, pictured, are on a trip to Wembley Stadium, London, circa 1950. They have been identified as G. Ashcroft, Mr. Aspinall, Sorry Tickle and J. Barlow.

Standish Celebrations for the Coronation of King George V1 in 1937. Tom Hughes is the King, with Miss B. Cowburn as Queen, and their pages are Allan Dawber and Jimmy Tomlinson.

Members of Standish Parish church bell ringers/choir, ready for a day out, circa 1930.

Eustace Chamberlain, Mr. Rankin, Ernest Fairclough and Canon Mellor, have been identified on this photograph taken before a day trip attended by the choir and bell ringers of Standish Parish church, circa 1935.

Standish Carnival, 1948.
This photograph shows Primrose Lane carnival float depicting a day at the seaside. Betty Hitchen, Julie Grady, Alan Turner and Billy Rhoden, are amongst the contestants, to win a prize for the best float.

A STANDISH MISCELLANY

The Limes

Edward Standish is mentioned in 1582 as the owner of Wigan Lane House, which became Limes Farm. The property was seized during the Civil War on the supposition that it belonged to Alexander Standish, son of the Lord of the Manor, who was a Colonel in the Royalist Army. The Limes was built in the grounds of Wigan Lane House, about the middle of the nineteenth century, as a residence for Thomas Taylor, J.P., who donated Wigan Public Library.

The Limes, Standish, circa 1920.

Close up view of the Limes, 1921.

Entry from the sales catalogue for Standish Estate, relating to the Limes, 1921.

CROOKE HALL, CROOKE.

Crooke Hall was built near to the River Douglas in 1608, for Peter and Elizabeth Catterall. The Leeds and Liverpool Canal was subsequently routed near to the old hall. Subsidence and serious flooding led to the demolition of the hall in 1937.

Crooke Hall, Crooke, circa 1900.

The Beeches, School Lane, Standish, circa 1920.

STANDISH WOODLANDS

There are many areas of woodland in the Standish district, which provided a retreat from the colliery grime. John Pit Wood was a particular favourite to enjoy the wonders of Mother Nature.

Views in John Pit Wood, circa 1915.

STREET SCENES

I find that topographical post card views, particularly street scenes, are amongst the most interesting, because they not only capture how things once were, but allow for comparison with present day. A number are included from the area.

This popular view of the 'Entrance to Standish' dates from about 1900,
and shows High Street at its junction with Church Street.

High Street, Standish, circa 1900. Standish Town Hall, which was built for the Local Board in 1893,
stands to the left of the photograph. It was eventually demolished in 1989.

Preston Road, Standish, circa 1900.

Preston Road, Standish, 1934.

Grove Lane, Standish, circa 1920.

Gathurst, circa 1930.

PRESBYTERIAN CHURCH, WRIGHTINGTON.

Tunley Presbyterian Chapel, is situated in Mossy Lea, Wrightington, and is one of the oldest in the country, having been originally built in 1691. The chapel is still in use.

Tunley Chapel, circa 1900.

Tunley Chapel, 2003.

Owd Thatch, Standish, circa 1900. Mrs. Swift is pictured at the door of her cottage, which stood next to Standish Conservative Club. It was demolished in 1928.

During the General Strike of 1926, there was much civil unrest and special constables were appointed to augment the regular police force. This certificate was awarded to Mr. Morgan of Grove Lane, Standish, who acted in the capacity of a special constable during this difficult period.

WE DESIRE on behalf of His Majesty's Government to thank you in common with all others who came forward so readily during the crisis and gave their services to the Country in the capacity of Special Constables.

Stanley Baldwin
PRIME MINISTER.

W Joynson Hicks
HOME SECRETARY.

Downing Street,
May, 1926.

To Leonard Morgan.

LANCASHIRE SPECIAL CONSTABULARY.

CHANGE AND DECAY

It is difficult to imagine what changes have taken place down the years, most are for the better but it is always sad to see familiar landmarks disappear. This series of photographs show the demolition of the Wheatsheaf public house and J.B.Almond's Brewery. Somerfield supermarket was subsequently built on the site.

APPENDIX 1

"AT THE GOING DOWN OF THE SUN AND IN THE MORNING, WE WILL REMEMBER THEM".

There are several war memorials in the Standish area to honour the fallen of two World Wars. It is extremely important that we do not forget the sacrifice they made.

Standish War Memorial is situated at the junction of Church Street and High Street. The Peace Gate at Standish Church contains a number of memorials, and St. Marie's Church also has its own cenotaph, which was recently removed to the opposite side of the church. Shevington's war memorial is situated on the village green, and was dedicated on the 9th November 1952.

The details of the inscription on the Peace Gate, are as follows, "To the Greater Glory of God. Amen. This memorial gate was built as a tribute to the men of Standish who, counting death no loss, valiantly made the last sacrifice in defence of their hearths and homes in the European War 1914-1918". The men, "Whose praise is throughout all the churches". "Who stands if freedom falls. Who dies if England lives". Kipling.

> Sons of the place let this of you be said
> That you who live are worthy of your dead
> These gave their lives that you who live may reap
> A richer harvest ere we fall asleep.   BOYD

The Peace Gate at Standish Church, 2003.

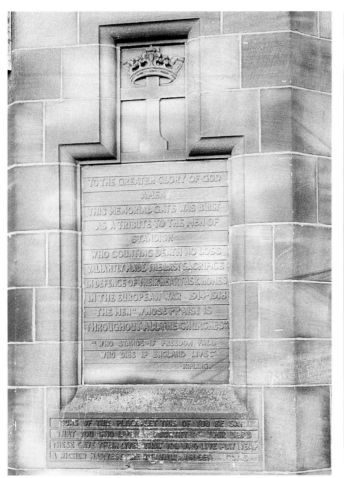

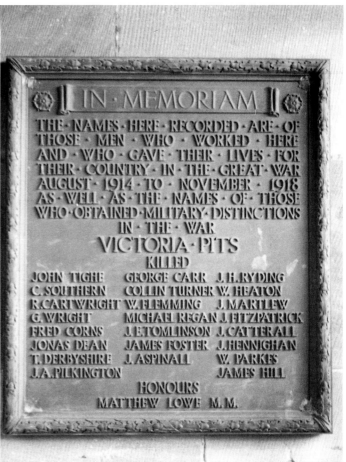

IN · MEMORIAM

THE · NAMES · HERE · RECORDED · ARE · OF
THOSE · MEN · WHO · WORKED · HERE
AND · WHO · GAVE · THEIR · LIVES · FOR
THEIR · COUNTRY · IN · THE · GREAT · WAR
AUGUST · 1914 · TO · NOVEMBER · 1918
AS · WELL · AS · THE · NAMES · OF · THOSE
WHO · OBTAINED · MILITARY · DISTINCTIONS
IN · THE · WAR

VICTORIA · PITS

KILLED

JOHN TIGHE	GEORGE CARR	J.H.RYDING
C.SOUTHERN	COLLIN TURNER	W. HEATON
R.CARTWRIGHT	W.FLEMMING	J.MARTLEW
G.WRIGHT	MICHAEL REGAN	J.FITZPATRICK
FRED CORNS	J.E.TOMLINSON	J.CATTERALL
JONAS DEAN	JAMES FOSTER	J.HENNIGHAN
T.DERBYSHIRE	J.ASPINALL	W. PARKES
J.A.PILKINGTON		JAMES HILL

HONOURS

MATTHEW LOWE M.M.

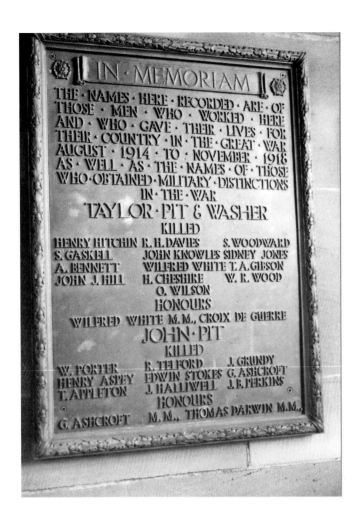

IN·MEMORIAM

THE·NAMES·HERE·RECORDED·ARE·OF
THOSE·MEN·WHO·WORKED·HERE
AND·WHO·GAVE·THEIR·LIVES·FOR
THEIR·COUNTRY·IN·THE·GREAT·WAR
AUGUST·1914·TO·NOVEMBER·1918
AS·WELL·AS·THE·NAMES·OF·THOSE
WHO·OBTAINED·MILITARY·DISTINCTIONS
IN·THE·WAR

TAYLOR·PIT & WASHER

KILLED

HENRY HITCHIN	R. H. DAVIES	S. WOODWARD
S. GASKELL	JOHN KNOWLES	SIDNEY JONES
A. BENNETT	WILFRED WHITE	T. A. GIBSON
JOHN J. HILL	H. CHESHIRE	W. E. WOOD
	O. WILSON	

HONOURS

WILFRED WHITE M.M., CROIX DE GUERRE

JOHN·PIT

KILLED

W. PORTER	R. TELFORD	J. GRUNDY
HENRY ASPEY	EDWIN STOKES	G. ASHCROFT
T. APPLETON	J. HALLIWELL	J. B. PERKINS

HONOURS

G. ASHCROFT M.M., THOMAS DARWIN M.M.

IN·MEMORIAM

THE·NAMES·HERE·RECORDED·ARE
THOSE·MEN·WHO·WORKED·H
AND·WHO·GAVE·THEIR·LIVES
THEIR·COUNTRY·IN·THE·GREAT·W
AUGUST·1914·TO·NOVEMBER·1
AS·WELL·AS·THE·NAMES·OF·TH
WHO·OBTAINED·MILITARY·DISTINCTIO
IN·THE·WAR

GIANTS·HALL·PIT

KILLED

JOHN TELFORD	J. DEARDEN	W. HOLLAN
THOMAS FINCH	J. PHILLIPS	H. GAMBLES
	W. CARTER	

HONOURS

SAMUEL·HENRY·GRIFFITHS M. M.
JAMES PHILLIPS M. M. W. CARTER D. C. M.
ISAAC JOLLEY M. M. J. GRIMSHAW D.

NAMES APPEARING ON ST.WILFRID'S PARISH CHURCH 'PEACE GATE'

Praise God for the members of Standish Parish Church who fell in the Great War
1914 - 1918

Amos Allen
Alfred Arstall
Charles F. Asbrey
Arthur Babb
Daniel Ball
Robert Banks
Robert G. Bentham
George W. Bibby
James Bibby
Thomas Bretherton
Frederick B. Brown
Hance Cain
Hugh Calderbank
John Campbell
Samuel Carpenter
Albert Crompton
Alexander Cush
Kenneth Dean
James Duckworth
John Eccleston
William A. Farrell
Thomas Farrimond
Walter Farrimond
Walter Farrington
John Ferrie
John Fisher
Edward Forshaw
William Grant
John Gray
J. Alfred Gregory
Peter Green
James Hale
James Harrison
Joseph W. Harrison
Wilfrid Harrison
William Hart (A).
William Hart (B).
Thomas Hill
James Hill
Seth J. Houghton

Roland Holland
Richard Hulme
Arthur Jennings
Harold Latham
Joseph Lewis
George Littlewood
Alfred Lowton
Joseph Lythgoe
Roland E. Maddison
Frank S. Marrow
Joseph Marsden
James Martlew
Charles Mather
Robert L. McCartney
Thomas Moncrief
Lord Moss
Bertie Norris
John Norris
Samuel Norris
Joseph Orrell
Walter W. Parks
John Pennington
John A. Pilkington
William Pitts
Ernest L. Porter
James Preston
Joseph Richardson
John H. Robinson
Peter Sheffield
James Smith
John A. Sutherland
John E. Tomlinson
Richard Tomlinson
Harold Topping
Moses Valentine
Edmund Wilding
Alexander Yates
Thomas Wass

List of the fallen during the 1939-1945 War

William Roy Armer
Ernest Aspey
John Astley
Robert Banks
Norman Barnes
David Booth
Victor Charles Bradshaw
Ernest Buckley
John Thomas Butterworth
Herbert Cornish
James Stephen Culshaw
James Owen Davies
Norman Thomas Duxbury
Clifford Alexander Farrimond
Eric Farrimond
James Thomas Finch
George Leslie Gore
Joseph Thomas Goulding
George Clifford Grundy
Arthur Noel Hampson
Leslie Holding
Henry Stephen Jacques
Arthur Jacques
William Johnson

Henry Langton
Robert Lowton
Harry Oliver Lloyd
Fred Lythgoe
Herbert Marsden
William Mason
Thomas Mather
Daniel Morrison
Nathan Robinson
John Grindrod Ruddick
Kenneth Seddon
Harry Sharrock
Thomas Sharrock
William James Cumberland
Shorrocks
Arthur Stanley Smith
Ernest Lawrence Snape
Harry Speakman
James Taylor
Alan Tige
James Richard Webster
Walter Whitter
Stanley Worthington
John Wyatt

St. Marie of the Annunciation Roman Catholic Church
List of the fallen during the 1914-1918 War

James Duffy
Thomas Duffy
William Halsall
Austin Heyes
Joseph Harrison
James Hennighan
James Foster

Thomas Regan
Oswald Wilson
Richard Hooton
Joseph Houghton
Cuthbert A.Marsh
Thomas Francis Livesey

Who gave their lives in the European War 1914-1918,
And to cherish whose memory, this cross is erected by their fellow parishioners and friends.
MAY THEY REST IN PEACE

On a comparison of the names included on the Peace Gate at Standish Church, and the War Memorial outside the Globe Hotel in Standish, there are the following differences.

1914 - 1918

Names on the Peace Gate omitted from the Standish War Memorial	Names on the Standish War Memorial omitted from the Peace Gate
Charles F. Asbrey	Frederick S. Brown
Robert Banks	Gerald B. Brown
Robert G. Bentham	Robert Danks
James Bibby	Kenneth J. Dean
Frederick B. Brown	Fred Fairhurst
Hugh Calderbank	Harold Fairhurst
John Campbell	Joseph Farrimond
Albert Crompton	* James Foster
Alexander Cush	Thomas Gaskell
Walter Farrimond	Thomas Gladman
John Fisher	* William Halsall
Peter Green	* James Hennighan
James Hale	* Austin G. Heyes
Wilfrid Harrison	William Holland
Thomas Hill	Ernest Parker
Roland Holland	William Porter
Harold Latham	* Thomas Regan
Roland E. Maddison	Joseph H. Ryding
Joseph Marsden	Edwin Stokes
Robert L. McCartney	Joseph Wade
John Norris	
Ernest L. Porter	
Joseph Richardson	* Included on St. Marie's Church memorial.

Names on the Pcacc Gate omitted from the Standish War Memorial

Names on the Standish War Memorial omitted from the Peace Gate

William Roy Armer
Norman Barnes
David Booth
Herbert Cornish
Norman Thomas Duxbury
Clifford Alexander Farrimond
Eric Farrimond
George Leslie Gore
Arthur Noel Hampson
Leslie Holding
Arthur Jacques
Henry Langton
Harry Oliver Lloyd
Fred Lythgoe
Daniel Morrison
Nathan Robinson
Ernest Lawrence Snape
James Taylor
James Richard Webster
John Wyatt

Leslie Booth
John Brannon
Henry Fairhurst
James Foster
Thomas Hilton
William Lythgoe
Thomas Wilson

Roburite Home Guard
Back row left to right: Bob Gordon (Springfield) Tom Little (Standish) Arnold Green(Gathurst)

Front row left to right: Jack McNally (Appley Bridge, Vicarage Ln) Fred Edge (Scotsman)
Robt Crawford (Denaby, Yorks) Percy Cleather (Loyals Regt) Joe Cowan(St Helens)

Shevington War Memorial

1914 - 1918

Thomas Jackson

John James Hill

Richard Hooton

Harry Kitchen

Frederick Hodge

Edward Dean

Robert G. Bentham

John Grundy

John Marshall

Robert H. Davies

William Halton

William Holland

Edward Stopforth

Oswald Wilson

Harry R. Taylor

1939 - 1945

James Lamb

Joseph Fitzpatrick

John E. Rigby

John Randall

Colin F. Coppock

Eric Lyon

Frank W. Highton

Cyril Haig

John McNamara

John H. Holcroft

Ernest L. Snape

Harry Mayers

Alan Paul T. Henry

Independent Order of Oddfellows Memorial, Standish

The Loyal Earl of Surrey Lodge in Standish, planted a tree near to Standish war memorial in 1910 to honour fallen members of the order. The tree was removed in 1958 and replaced with a stone monument on which a plaque was mounted.

APPENDIX 2

There follow details of the Mannex Directory of 1866 and Kelly's Directory for 1923, relating to the Standish district.

STANDISH PARISH

Extends from the parish of Chorley to that of Wigan, and from Eccleston to Bolton-le-Moors, comprises an area of about 15,000 acres, and is refreshed by the rivers Douglas and Yarrow and the rivulet called Bradley Brook. It is intersected by the Leeds and Liverpool Canal, and the London and North-Western line of railway. Standish parish is a highly interesting and populous district. Coal and cannel mining is carried on very extensively, the steam engines used in the collieries being of the aggregate power of about 1200 horses. The population of the parish in 1801 amounted to 5489; 1821, 7617; 1841, 9686; and 1861 to 10,410; the registrar's district in the latter year containing 6894 souls. Standish parish is divided into the ten townships of Standish-with-Langtree, Adlington, Anderton, Charnock Heath, Charnock Richard, Coppull, Duxbury, Shevington, Welch Whittle, and Worthington.

STANDISH-WITH-LANGTREE has a village on elevated ground, three miles N.N.W. from Wigan. The name has given rise to various conjectures, but all vague and unsatisfactory. In the arms of the family of Standish, three plates, anciently called stand-dishes, are represented. Most likely the name has some reference to *Stone*, from the Anglo-Saxon *Stan*. Dr. Whitaker says, Standish was one of the twelve considerable towns in the south of Lancashire, in which the Saxons erected fortified castles, for the residences of their chiefs and the protection of the country. It belonged to a family of the local name soon after the conquest, but to enter into the history of this ancient family would occupy too much of our space. In the reign of Richard II. the honour of knighthood was conferred on Rafe Standish for the assistance rendered in suppressing the insurrection of Wat Tyler and Jack Straw, and in 1482 Sir Alexander Standish was created a baronet for his heroism in the battle of Hutton Field. His second son, Dr. Henry Standish, was bishop of Asaph, and assisted Queen Catherine in her defence against the pains and penalties of Henry VIII. He was also guardian of the Franciscan Convent in London, and provincial of his order, and was a dignitary of great learning and piety. John Standish, a celebrated polemical writer, and one of the most determined opponents to the change of religion in this country, was born here. Standish Hall, an ancient brick edifice, had been for a length of time the residence of the Standish family, but in 1825 Charles Standish quitted the mansion and went to reside on the continent. The hall is now the property of Lionel Standish, Esq., who resides on the continent, and is occupied by Nathaniel Eckersley, Esq. Attached to the hall is an ancient *Catholic Chapel*, of which the Rev. W. P. Corlett is pastor. Here is also a Catholic school, attended by about 90 children. The *Church* of St. Wilfrid is a large handsome structure, consisting of nave, side aisles, chancel, and tower, terminating in a spire. It is of the Tuscan order, and the exterior exhibits two tiers of castellated battlements and pinnacles. The interior is elevated; the nave is divided from the side aisles by seven arches on each side, upheld by Tuscan columns with square capitals; and the arch between the nave and chancel has a noble span, and is finely proportioned. The church was rebuilt in 1584, by the first Protestant rector, but a parish church existed here as early as 1291. Amongst the tablets and monuments may be mentioned a splendid marble one executed by Bacon, at a cost of £1600, whereon is delineated the figure of commerce. The benefice is a rectory, worth about £2000 per annum. The adowson has been in the Standish family for more than seven centuries. It is now in the gift of Lionel Standish, Esq., and the Rev. William Harper Brandreth, M.A., is the rector. The church has been considerably restored during the incumbency of the present rector, and several memorial windows have been presented. The *Free Grammar School* founded in 1603, possesses an endowment of about £70 a year, and is now efficiently conducted by Mr. Alexander Richardson; average attendance 100. The school is under Government inspection, and the house has lately been repaired. *Mary Smalley's School for Girls* was founded in 1794, when that benevolent lady left £1000 for its endowment. The annual income is about £20, for which 20 girls are taught free. The generous founder, who was niece to the Rev. Edward Smalley, M.A., rector of the parish, also left several other charities, the record of many of which is preserved on a tablet in the church. Two fairs are held here annually—on the 29th of June and 25th of November; and in the township are several collieries, all except one the property of the Wigan Coal and Iron Company, Limited. Here is also an extensive *Paper Mill*, worked by

Messrs. J. and T. B. Crompton, and large *Brick and Tile Works* belonging to Mr. James Partington. Langtree was formerly styled a manor. *Bradley Hall* and *Langtree Hall* are ancient buildings in Langtree, the former occupied by the Messrs. Fisher, coal proprietors. Population of the township in 1861, 3054. Rateable value, £17,574; gross rental, £19,188. In the centre of the village is an ancient relic, consisting of a single cross shaft springing from a tier of steps; and contiguous to the village are the remains of several crosses. Thorn Hill is a pleasant range of good houses in this township, occupied by Wigan tradesmen. Standish is now supplied with gas by the Wigan Gas Co.

Standish-with-Langtree Township.

POST-OFFICE at Mr. John Fisher's. Letters through Wigan.

Almond Mary, grocer
Ambrose Peter, corn miller, Jolly Mill
Aspinall James, gentleman
Atherton Robert, beerhouse
Atherton George, vict. Eagle & Child

Bailey Edw. clog and shoemaker
Bailey John, painter
Ball Henry, vict. Royal Oak
Barker John, plumber and glazier
Barton Matthew, Esq., Effingham Hs.

Bentham Henry, grocer and butcher
Bentham James, shopkeeper
Bentham Stephen, grocer
Bentham Thomas, grocer
Bentham William, shopkeeper
Berry Mr. William
Birley Mr. Frederick, Highfield
Booth Dennis, blacksmith
Brandreth Rev. William Harper, M.A. rector
Bradley Hall Coal Co.— Benj. Fisher, proprietor
Bromilow Robert, watchmaker
Brookes Edw. boot and shoemaker
Catholic School—Mary Sloane
Chadwick Wm. auctioneer & appraiser
Chamberlain Jas. painter & plasterer
Chamberlain Mary, beerhouse
Cooper Peter, beerhouse
Collier Edward, painter, plumber, and glazier
Collier Richard, boot and shoemaker
Corlett Rev. W. P. (Catholic) The Hermitage
Craston Mr. Anthony, Thorn hill
Crompton John and Thomas B. paper mfrs.—Solomon Horrocks, manager
Darbyshire Thos. vict. Original Seven Stars
Darbyshire Peter, upholsterer
Dickinson William, wheelwright
Duckworth Richard, vict. Black Bull
Eckersley Nathaniel, Esq. J.P. Standish Hall
Ellam Matthew, colliery & land agent
Endowed School (girls)—Eliz. Hoggarth and Mary Harrison
Evans Rev. Henry, B.A. curate
Fisher Benj. coal proprtr. Bradley Hall
Finch John, beerhouse
Finch Robert, nailmaker and shopkpr.
Foster John, tailor
Foster Mary, shopkeeper
France John, clogger
Freeman Jn. S. land agt. Prospect hill
Gaskell James, gentleman
Gaskell Thomas, bookkeeper
Gillibrand John, grocer and draper
Gillibrand Robert, grocer and draper
Gore George, shopkeeper
Gorton James, beerhouse
Grammar School—Alex. Richardson, head master; Chas. N. Richardson, second master
Grundy Miss
Hains Rev. Philip, Thorn hill
Halsall Robert, beerhouse
Halton Dennis, fishmonger
Halton James, vict. New Seven Stars

Halton Thomas, vict. Black Horse
Harmer Esther, grocer
Harrison Thomas, station master
Heyes William, vict. Wheat Sheaf Inn
Hunter J. L. Esq., C.E. The Grove
Jones Charles, colliery agent
Kershaw Mr. George
Kirkham William, carrier to Wigan
Lancaster John, Esq. Fields
Leader Mr. William, Langtree Cottage
Leigh Charles, beerhouse
Liptrot John, beerhouse
Lloyd Abraham, bone manure manufr.
Lyon Elizabeth, shopkeeper
Marsden Joshua, joiner
Martland Thomas, sanitary inspector
Martland William, assistant overseer
Mason Richard, beerhouse
Moss Henry, shoemaker
Moss Peter, shoemaker
Parkinson Mr. Peter
Partington James, brick and tile manufacturer
Pendlebury Roger, clogger
Pendlebury James, clogger
Pennington James, clay pipe maker
Pilkington Ann, dressmaker
Pilkington John, vict. Boar's Head
Price Mrs. Mary
Price John Llewellyn, surgeon and registrar of births and deaths
Richardson Thomas, miller
Rideout W. J. (Crompton John and Thomas B.) paper manufacturer
Ryder William, grocer
Schofield Peter, vict. Waggon Horse
Sharples Mrs. Ellen
Simm Esther, milliner
Simm John, nailmaker
Simm Richard, painter
Simm Thomas, beerhouse
Simm Thomas, grocer and painter
Smethurst Arthur Clough, Esq. The Limes
Smith Henry, joiner and builder
Smith Thomas, excise officer
Snape Mr. Charles, Thorn hill
Stopford Mrs. Mary, White hall
Stopforth Miss Ann
Stubbs Samuel, grocer
Swift George, butcher
Swift Mary, shopkeeper
Taylor John, coal proprietor, Strickland houses
Thompson Mr. Robert, Thorn hill
Turner William, beerhouse
Tyrer John, tailor
Walker Mr. Edward Ross, Thorn hill
Walton Thomas, shopkeeper

Watkinson William, plumber & glazier
Watmough James, beerhouse
Wigan Coal and Iron Co. (Limited) colliery proprietors ; Hugh Mc. Donald, manager
Wilding Mary Ann, milliner
Wilding John, saddler
Wilson John, beerhouse
Woodcock Edward, Esq. Thorn hill

Farmers

Ainscough James
Ambrose John
Ambrose Peter
Ashhurst Thomas, Langtree hall
Astley Philip
Ball Edward
Ball Margaret
Bond Richard
Bullen Charlotte, Fairhurst house
Chadwick William
Charnock Jane, Grove
Dickinson John
Duckworth Lewis, Limbrick house
Duckworth Richard, Bank house
Ellison Enoch
Fisher Richard (yeoman) Bradley hall
Gaskell William

Gill Robert
Gill Jacob
Gill Thomas
Halton William
Hilton Betty
Lea Thomas
Liptrot Henry and Thomas
Orrell Richard
Prescott Robert
Richardson William
Richardson Thomas
Scotson James
Seddon John
Speakman Misses
Sutton Henry
Sutton James, Dam house
Sutton Robert
Swift John
Swift Thomas
Swift William
Taylor Richard, Langtree old hall
Walker Thomas
Walton Thomas
Waring Thomas
Weston John
Wignall Thomas
Wilson Richard

WORTHINGTON is anothr small township, four miles north from Wigan, containing only 678a. 0r. 33p., including nearly 21 acres of road, and its population in 1801 was 111 ; 1821, 143 ; 1841, 133 ; and 1861, 133. Rateable value £2200. The principal landowners are the Clayton and Cardwell families. In 1588, a family of the local name resided at the hall, which was built in 1577. Of this family was Dr. Thomas Worthington, who was educated at the English college of Douay, and was the author of "Comments on the English Testament," printed at Rheims. On coming over to England he was taken and sent to the tower ; but was soon after liberated, on condition to leave the country. *North Hall* was built about the middle of the last century, by Lord Chief Justice Clayton, of Adlington, as a seat for his brother. It is now occupied by Edward Silvester, Esq., J.P. A reservoir, now in formation for the town of Wigan, is partly situated in this township, and partly in that of Haigh. It is 500 yards long, 180 yards broad, and 45 feet deep, and will be capable of holding 120,000,000 gallons of water ; J. L. Hunter, Esq., engineer.

Worthington Township Directory.

Alker William, blacksmith
Dickinson James, wherlwright
Digby Charles, vict. White Crow
Silvester Edw. Esq. J.P. North Hall

Farmers

Ainsworth Henry
Dickinson Thomas

Hampson John
Hampson Mary
Irlam William
Mort Mary
Ollerton Jane
Ollerton Peter
Watkinson John, Worthington Hall

SHEVINGTON, as the name implies, is situate on the declivity of an eminence, 3 miles W.N.W. from Wigan, and extends to the north bank of the river Douglas. The name may be derived from the British word *cefn*, meaning the back or ridge of a mountain, and the Anglo Saxon *ton*, a village, &c. In ancient times it gave name to a family of the Schevyngtons; and it appears that Richard Schevynton gave a tract of land here, with common pasture, to Burscough Priory. The principal land owners now are Sir Thomas George Hesketh, Bart., M.P., and Thomas Dicconson, Esq.; the former is lord of the manor. It contains 1700 acres, and its population in 1801, was 646; 1821, 836; 1841, 1122; and 1861, 1115. Rateable value, £7280; gross rental, £7947. There are several extensive coal mines in this township. The *Unitarians* have a chapel here, enlarged in 1831. There is a *National*

School, and house for the master, erected by subscription in 1814. The school is now attended by about 60 children. In 1845, another school was erected here, by Edward Woodcock, Esq. Divine service is conducted at each school, alternately, every Sunday morning and afternoon, for which the clergyman receives the interest of £2000, left for that purpose by Mrs. and Miss Thickness; also £30 a year given by the rector of Standish, making the total salary £100. Holt farm was formerly the residence of Captain Holt, who was twice imprisoned in the bastile. Crook Hall was once the residence of the Pearsons; and Shevington Hall was inhabited, upwards of two centuries ago, by the Woodwards, who were seated here as late as the year 1701. White Hall bears the date of 1653, and was owned by the Baldwins. Finch Mill, another ancient place, was the secluded retreat of Edward Dicconson, Catholic bishop of Malensis, in the last century. On Shevington Moor is a causeway, called Cripplegate, which is said to have led to the house of two maiden ladies who gave alms to every crippled applicant, and from this circumstance to have taken its name.

Shevington Township Directory.

Barnes Thomas, beerhouse
Bassnett John, master of National School
Bell William, farm bailiff to T. Dicconson, Esq.
Bentham Henry, tailor
Bentham Nathan, shopkeeper
Bimpson Thomas, wheelwright
Brindle William, colliery proprietor and vict. Hesketh Arms
Cowley David, wheelwright
Davenport Thomas, beerhouse
Fairhurst John, beerhouse
Foster John, shopkeeper
Grime Henry, schoolmaster
Grounds James, shopkeeper
Heald Hugh, coal proprietor, Phœnix Colliery; R. Dickinson, manager
Hilton Alice, beerhouse
Holland Geo. vict. George and Dragon
Lea Edw. clog and shoemaker
Leigh John, beerhouse
Marsh Richard, beerhouse
Marsh William and Co. coal proprietors, Green Slate Collieries; John Redshaw, managing partner
Ratcliffe John, blacksmith
Rigby James, shopkeeper
Stopforth Richard, vict. Plough and Harrow

Tayleur John and Co. coal proprietors; h. New Hall Cottage
Wilding Edw. beerhouse

Farmers

Ambrose Ellis (and miller)
Barton Robert (and grocer)
Bimpson James
Bowling John
Brindle William
Bullen William
Danson Robert
Dawber Elizabeth
Fairclough William
Goulding Henry
Hilton Thomas
Hilton Margaret
Lang Edward
Orrell George
Mann Godfrey W. (& colliery manager)
Park Richard
Ratcliffe Mary
Shuffleton Joseph, Crook Hall
Silcock William
Taylor Thomas, White hill
Thompson Henry
Walmsley Richard
Williamson Samuel, Old hall
Woods Hugh

CHARNOCK RICHARD, about 2 miles S.W. from Chorley, contains 2000 acres, chiefly the property of Mrs. Alison and R. T. Parker, Esq.; and its population, in 1801, amounted to 587; 1821, 794; 1841, 784; and 1861, 899. Rateable value, £4784. The London and North-Western Railway runs through the township; and here are two extensive collieries: the coal working is what is generally termed the Mountain coal, which is found of good quality. *Park Hall*, an ancient mansion in this township, is the residence of Mrs. Alison, and is supposed to have once been occupied by the Hoghtons, of Hoghton Tower. Here is a neat *Church*, built in 1861, chiefly by James Darlington, Esq., who is patron of the living. The Rev. John Webster is the present incumbent. A *National School* was erected here in 1858.

Charnock Richard Township Directory.

Alison Mrs. Alice, Park hall
Alison Henry, Esq. Park hall
Barker James, vict. Dog and Partridge and coal proprietor, Pemberton House Colliery
Collier James, blacksmith
Cowling Thomas, grocer
Greaves Michael, grocer
Holmes Joseph, tailor
Lightoller Mr. Frederick James, Hill Cottage
Norris Hugh, shoemaker
Parker Thomas Townley, Esq. J.P.
Sephton William, vict. Bowling Green
Sherratt and Barker, coal proprietors, Royal Charter Colliery
Sherratt Thomas (Sherratt & Barker) h. Four lane ends
Smith Thomas, coal proprietor, Plymouth House
Webster Rev. John, incumbent
Whittle William, colliery surveyor, Alma House

Farmers
Barrow Richard

Berry Andrew
Calderbank James
Cocker William
Corner James
Corner Robert
Cropper Richard
Fowler John
Goulding David, Park hall farm
Goulding John, Old farm
Goulding Robert
Green Elizabeth
Greaves Michael
Lucas Thomas
Moorfield William
Morris James
Ormesher Robert
Phillipson Richard
Riding John
Sharples Alfred
Sharrock James
Swann John
Whittle Thomas
Yates Daniel

WELCH WHITTLE, a small township 3½ miles S.S.W. from Chorley, contains only 530 acres, mostly belonging to Thomas Dicconson, Esq.; and its population in 1801 was 127; 1821, 151; 1841, 149; and 1861, 148. Rateable value, £1822. Here are several collieries.

Welch Whittle Township Directory.

Darlington James, coal proprietor
Holmes John, wheelwright
Worthington Matth. vict. Hind's Head

Farmers
Edgeley William
Glover Richard
Glover William
Hart William
Hayes William

Hill Edmund
Holmes John
Iddon James
Makinson James
Marshall Edward
Rollins John
Stock Ann
Stringfellow James
Threlfall Alexander
Yates James

STANDISH is an extensive parish, township and village, on the old road from Wigan to Preston, with a station on the Wigan and Preston section of the London, Midland and Scottish railway, 3½ miles north from Wigan, 6 south from Chorley and 197 from London, in the Ince division of the county, Leyland hundred, Wigan union and county court district, petty sessional division of Leyland hundred, rural deanery of Leyland, archdeaconry of Blackburn and diocese of Manchester. The township of Standish-with-Langtree adopted the Local Government Act, 1858, October 11, 1872, but under the Local Government Act, 1894, it is now governed by an Urban District Council. The Wigan electric tramway system has been extended to this parish. The church of St. Wilfrid is a fine building of stone in the Transitional style, dating from 1291, and was rebuilt in 1584 by Richard Moodie, the first Protestant rector, when aisles and clerestories were added in the Perpendicular style: it consists of chancel, nave, aisles, south porch and a western tower containing a clock and 8 bells, some of which date from 1714 to 1846: there are 10 stained windows, including the east window, presented in the year 1850 by Mrs. Chisenhale, of Arley, and one on the south side, inserted by R. C. Browne Clayton esq. in memory of his only son, Lieut. Robert John Browne Clayton, who was mortally wounded in the attack on the Redan at Sebastopol Sept. 8th, 1855: in the church is an altar tomb, with a recumbent effigy of Richard Moodie, who is represented in his Franciscan habit, and there is also a memorial to Sir Edward Wrightington kt. of Wrightington, ob. 1658: the handsome oak screen, placed in the church at Easter, 1886, is a memorial to the Rev. Canon William Harper Brandreth M.A. 44 years rector of the parish, who died April 17th, 1885, and was erected by his children, as recorded on a brass tablet affixed on an adjoining pillar: the church was restored in 1859: a new organ was provided in 1913. The register dates from the year 1558. The living is a rectory, net yearly value £1,057, with 318 acres of glebe and residence, in the gift of Miss Mary Adams, and held since 1886 by the Rev. Charles William Newton Hutton M.A. of St. John's College, Cambridge: in the rectory grounds are some venerable yews, said to be 600 years old. The Roman Catholic church, dedicated to St. Mary, and opened 17th May, 1884, is a plain building of brick, consisting of nave, aisles and a church turret containing one bell, and will seat 500 persons: church rooms and a presbytery were added in 1907. There is a Wesleyan chapel, built 1897, and seating 250, and a Primitive Methodist chapel, erected in 1891, and also seating 250. There are very valuable and extensive mines of cannel and other coal. Standish Hall, an Elizabethan mansion, situated in a well-wooded park, is at present (1924) unoccupied. Henry Nouailles Widdrington Standish esq. is lord of the manor and principal landowner. The soil is clay; subsoil, clay, stone and coal. The chief crops are wheat and oats. The acreage of the township and Urban District of Standish-cum-Langtree is 3,266, of which 18 acres water; rateable value, £34,870; the population in 1921 was 7,293, and of the ecclesiastical parish in 1911, 6,959. The population of the Urban District wards in 1921 was:—North, 6,266; South, 1,027.

Parish Clerk, Richard Farramond.

Post, M. O., T. & Telephone Call Office, Standish.—Miss Esther Ann Gillibrand, sub-postmistress. Letters from Wigan

Post Office, Standish Lower Ground.—Miss Martha Halsall, sub-postmistress. Letters from Wigan. Woodhouse Lane is the nearest money order & Wigan the nearest telegraph office

WORTHINGTON is a small township in the parish of Standish, 1½ miles south-east from Coppull station on the Wigan and Preston section of the London, Midland and Scottish railway, a quarter of a mile north-east from Standish railway station and 4 miles north from Wigan. The Wigan Water Works are here. North Hall, erected about the year 1750, is occupied as a farm house. Richard Clayton esq. who is lord of the manor, and the trustees of Viscount Cardwell (d. 1886) are the chief landowners. The soil is clay and gravel; subsoil, sand and gravel. The chief crops are wheat and oats and pasturage. The area is 638 acres of land and 20 of water; rateable value, £5,258; the population in 1921 was 233.

Post Office, Worthington.—Florence Blatchford, sub-postmistress. Letters arrive from Wigan. Standish, 1 mile distant, is the nearest money order & telegraph office

STANDISH-WITH-LANGTREE URBAN DISTRICT COUNCIL.
Offices, High street.

Meeting day, 1st tuesday in every month at 4.30 p.m. & committee meetings, 3rd monday in every month at 4.30.

Members.
Chairman, Henry Fairhurst.
Vice-Chairman, Gerald Hewlett.

William Almond	Gerald Hewlett
John Thomas Baxter	George William Mather
John Brewer	Walter Smith
Luke Cunningham	Frank Stonehouse
Francis Edmund	Thomas Josiah Wright
Robert Finney	

Officers.

Clerk, Supt. Assistant Overseer & Accountant, John H. Richards, Council offices, High street
Collector, Richard Charnock, Council offices
Law Clerks, Ackerley & Son, solicitors, Wigan
Treasurer, David Goldsworth, Westminster Bank Ltd. Wigan
Medical Officer of Health, George Henry Ormsby L.M.S.S.A. Lond. 1 High street
Surveyor, Sanitary Inspector & Sewage Farm Manager, Alvin Clough, Council offices, High street
Waterman, William Lea, High street

—————

County Police Station, George Pearson, sergeant, & 4 constables

SCHOOLS.

The Grammar School was founded in 1603 by Dame Mary Langton, & the endowment was augmented in 1633 by the Rev. William Leigh & since then by other benefactors; the yearly income is now £100, arising from 137 acres of land; the school, enlarged in 1897, will now hold 356 scholars; the education is elementary: the school is managed by a board of 8 governors, of which the rector of Standish is chairman; Thomas Josiah Wright M.A. master

Public Elementary.

Standish (girls & infants), built in 1826, for 500 children & enlarged in 1891, for 643 children; Miss Edmondson, mistress; Miss Nesta Finch, infants' mistress
Standish Lower Ground (mixed), built 1895, for 168 children; Miss Mary Sweetlove, mistress
Roman Catholic (mixed & infants), built in 1860, enlarged in 1896, for 300 children; Miss Margaret Ann Foster, mistress; Mrs. McLarney, infants' mistress

RAILWAY STATIONS.

Standish, Albert Victor Wray, station master
Boar's Head Junction, Arthur John Prudon, station master

—————

Electric Trams to & from Wigan every twenty minutes

STANDISH.

PRIVATE RESIDENTS.

Ainsworth William Gladstone, Rookwood
Appleton Charles, Bradley hall
Arrowsmith Harry, 34 Chorley road
Bentham Ernest, Broomfield
Bentham Josiah, Thornhill
Derbyshire Richard Aaron, Langtree cot
Dewse Wm. W. Oak Dene, Thornhill
Edmonds Frederick, The Grove
Ellis Henry Ratcliffe, The Knoll
Healy John, Thornhill
Hewitt John, Thornhill
Hewlett Gerald, Highfield house
Hutton Rev. Charles William Newton M.A. (rector), The Rectory
Kinch Walter Somerville J.P. The Limes
Noble John, The Mount
Norris Rev. James (Roman Catholic), The Presbytery
Ormsby George Henry, 1 High street
Parker Miss, Beckside, Rectory lane
Partington James, 199 Preston road
Richards John H. Deyne bank, Wigan rd
Rigby Mrs. Briarcroft
Scott-Barratt Henry Augustus, Mere oaks
Shaw T. Wilson. Rodenhurst, Church st
Sole Frederick William, 3 Chorley road
Stanislaw Barron, Prospect house
Starr Edward H. Laurel bank, Chorley rd
Starr William H. Holly bank, Chorley rd
Sumner Harold O.B.E., J.P. Ashfield ho
Waddington Miss, Thornhill
Ward Rev. Geo.A.,M.A.(curate),Rectory la
Ward James, 36 Chorley road
Whalley James, Holly bank
Wilding Edward, Clifton vils. School lane
Wright Thomas Josiah M.A. (master of Endowed Grammar School)
Wrigley John Arthur, Douglas house
Yates James, Wigan road

COMMERCIAL.

Abbott Wm. ironmonger, 41 Preston road
Allen Amos, shopkeeper, 1 Rectory lane
Almond James B. brewer, Standish brewery. T A " Almond;" T N 10
Ashbrook Annie (Mrs.), grocer, 12 Chorley road
Ashcroft John, farmer, High street
Ashton Thos. frmr. Thompson House farm
Aspinall Moses & Co. grocers, Standish Lower ground
Aspinall Peter, shopkeeper, 16 High st
Baldwin Thomas, farmer, Rose Hill farm
Baron Joseph, boot & shoe dlr. 18 Pole st
Bateson Joseph, butcher, High street
Baxter Richard, builder, Almond Brook rd
Bentham Albert, shopkeeper, 62 High st
Bentham Ernest, cattle dlr. Broomfield ho
Bentham John, shopkeeper, 6 Preston rd
Bingham William Henry, excise & pension officer, Almond Bank
Blackledge Robert, painter, see Hurst & Blackledge
Bradley Manufacturing Co. Limited (A. W. Noble, manager), cotton spinners & manufactrs. T N 6
British & Argentine Meat Co. Limited, butchers, Preston road
Brooks & Devine, farmers, Dam House fm
Brown Peter, plumber, 37 Church street
Burt Mary (Mrs.), Pack Horse P.H. Almond bank
Castelli Charles, farmer,Grunnell Fold fm
Chadwick Alice (Mrs.),butchr.69 Church st
Charnock Richard, estate agent, Cross st
Clarke Andrew, Old Seven Stars P.H. Preston road
Clarkson William, beer ret. 23 School lane
Clough Alvin, surveyor, sanitary inspector & sewage farm manager, Council offices, High street
Cockram John, ironmonger, Preston road
Cockram Thomas, shopkeeper, 22 High st
Cooper & Nelmes, confectnrs. 12 High st
Cunliffe Edward, insur. agt. 5 Church ter
Danson John, St.Patrick's inn,149Prestn.rd
Dawler William, 19 Church street
Day Thomas, clogger, Standish Lower ground
Demings James, hair dresser,7 Preston rd
Dobson William Henry, farmer, Roundmoor & Wakefield farms
Dunn Thomas, farmer, Standish Lower ground
Eastham James, shopkeeper, Market st
Fairhurst Harry, fruiterer & greengrocer, Preston road
Fairhurst Harry, greengrocer,59 Preston rd
Fairhurst Henry, grocer, 28 Preston road
Fairhurst James, grocer, 1 School lane
Fairhurst Joseph, butcher, 42 Preston rd
Farrimond John H. butcher,126 Preston rd
Farrimond Thos. greengro. 151 Preston rd
Finch Henry, farmer, Robin hill
Foster Louis, clogger, 15 High street
Gerrard Mary (Miss), grocer, 68 High st
Gill Joseph, farmer, Giants hall, Standish Lower ground
Gillibrand Esther Ann (Miss), grocer, & sub-post office, 37 High street
Gobin Joseph, Boar's Head P.H.Wigan rd
Gorton Joseph, saddler, 1 Preston road
Grant Edward, cinema hall, Market street
Gray George, grocer, 181 Preston road
Gregory Roger, grocer. 52 High street
Gregson James, hair drssr. 144 Preston rd
Gregson Thos. hair dresser, 61 High st
Hale Samuel, grocer, 1 Market place
Higham Charles, Royal Oak P.H.Standish Lower ground
Higham Thomas, farmer
Hilton Thos. farmer, Standish Lower grnd
Holding Thomas, confectioner, High st
Hooson Joseph, clogger, 44 High street
Howard John & Son,butchers, High street
Hulme Humphry, beer retlr. 98 High st
Hulme James, shopkeeper, Bradley lane
Hurst & Blackledge,painters & decorators, 23 Standish Lower ground
Jennings Catherine (Mrs.), shopkeeper, 34 Preston road
Jones Geo. pawnbroker, 9 & 11 Preston rd
Lewis Frank, shopkpr. 74 Preston road
Lewis John, farmer, The Limes farm, Wigan road
Liptrot James, joiner, Wigan road
Lucas Catherine (Mrs.), grocer, 81 High st
Maiden William Henry, draper, High st
Martlew John Thomas, farmer, Standish Lower ground
Mason T. & R. cloggers, 71a, Church st
Mather George William, Black Horse P.H. 7 Church street
Meadow Dairy Co. Ltd. grocers, 4b,High st
Moore William, beer retailer, 1 Wigan la
Naylor Arth. E.Wheatsheaf P.H.Preston rd
Nicholas Isaac, farmer, Bradley Hall frm
Ormsby George Henry L.M.S.S.A.Lond. physician & surgeon, & medical officer of health to the Urban District Council, 1 High street
Peers Alexander, farmer, Preston road
Peers Ebenezer, farmer, Lark Hill farm
Peers Joseph, farmer, Besses Well farm
Pennington Thomas, grocer. 5 & 6 High st
Rainford James, shopkpr. 13 Market pl
Richards John H. supt. assistant overseer, accountant & clerk to the Urban District Council & registrar of births & deaths for Standish sub-district, High street
Robinson William, shopkeeper, The Grove
Rothwell David, beer retlr. 73 High st
Rushton O. & G. Limited, grocers, Preston road & Standish Lower ground
Sherlock Herbert, blacksmith
Simm William, blacksmith, Preston road
Smallshaw Robert, beer retailer, Standish Lower ground
Smith Alice (Mrs.), shopkeepr. Market pl
Smith Patrick, boot & shoe maker, 169 Preston road

Speakman Mathias, Black Bull P.H. Market place
Standish Bakery Co. bakers, High street
Standish Conservative Club Buildings Co. Limited (John Ryding, sec)
Standish Endowed Grammar School (Thos. Josiah Wright M.A. master)
Taylor Jas. frmr. Standish Lower ground
Thew Thos. frmr.Barker's farm,Chorley rd
Turner Jane (Mrs.), grocer, Preston road
Turner John, poor law relieving officer
Turner Robert J. wheelwright, High st
Unsworth Philip, shopkeeper, Bradley la
Vernon Harry, farmer, Walker's farm
Walsh Thomas, draper, 11 & 12 Market pl
Walton Samuel, farmer, Langtree farm
Wareing Samuel, farmer, Brockhurst, Lower ground
Watkinson Annie (Mrs.), grocer, 110 Preston road
Welch John, farmer, Pepper lane
Westminster Bank Ltd. (sub-branch) (open wed. & sat.), Council chambers, High street; draw on head office, 41 Lothbury, London E C 2
Wigan Coal & Iron Co. Limited (Francis Edmond, manager), Prospect colliery
Wigan & District Equitable Co-operative Society Limited, Preston rd. & Standish Lower ground
Wilding Harriett (Mrs.),news agt.High st
Wilding Tom, motor engineer, 63 & 65 High street
Williams Deacon's Bank Limited (subbranch to Wigan, mon. & fri. 10.30 a.m. till 2 p.m.), 2 High street; draw on London office, 20 Birchin lane E C 3. **See advertisement on outside Top & Bottom Edges**
Wilson Herbert, chemist, 8 High street
Winstanley Thos. shopkpr. Lower grounds

WORTHINGTON.

PRIVATE RESIDENTS.

Lawrence Edward J.P. Worthington lodge
Young Alexander, Kilney court

COMMERCIAL.

Alker William, farmer, Rennald's farm
Arrowsmith John, shopkeeper
Bentham Ernest, White Cow inn
Blatchford Florence (Miss), shopkeeper & sub-postmistress
Dicconson Mary Ann (Mrs.), wheelwright
Donald Robert Buchan, engineer Wigan Corporation Water works
Edmondson Thos. farmer,Worthington hall
Edmondson Thomas, jun. farmer, North Hall farm
Glover James, farmer, Gorse hall
Hodge Henry, farmer, Talbot House farm
Mort Thomas & Arnold, farmers, Black Lawyer's farm
Ollerton George, farmer, Smalley's farm
Reece William, Crown P.H
Rigby Charles (Mrs.), farmer, Boar's farm
Rigby William, farmer, Mill bridge
Standish (The) Co. Ltd. Standish bleach & dye works (telegrams to Bleach works, Standish). T N 566 Wigan
Walton Thos. Waring, farmer, Bibby's frm
Wigan Corporation Water Works (Robert Buchan Donald, engineer), Arley

SHEVINGTON is a township and parish, formed Jan. 17, 1873, from the parish of Standish, and comprises Shevington, Crooke and Gathurst, being 3 miles north-west from Wigan, in the Ince division of the county, Leyland hundred, petty sessional division of Leyland hundred, union and county court district of Wigan, rural deanery of Leyland, archdeaconry of Blackburn and diocese of Manchester. The Leeds and Liverpool canal runs through the township and the river Douglas divides it from Orrell. The church of St. Anne, erected in 1887 at a cost of £2,000, is a structure of brick in the Early English style, and consists of chancel, nave and a small western turret containing one bell: there are 268 sittings. The register dates from the year 1887. The living is a vicarage, net yearly value £335, with residence, in the gift of the rector of Standish, and held since 1900 by the Rev. George Blagden Hopkins. At Shevington Moor is a Primitive Methodist chapel, built in 1910. The charities are distributed in clothing. Near Appley Bridge are the works of the Grove Chemical Co. Limited. The soil is clay; subsoil, marl. The chief crops are wheat and oats, with some pasture land. The area is 1,698 acres of land and 29 of water; rateable value, £8,566; the population in 1921 was 1,949 in the township, and of the ecclesiastical parish in 1911, 3,475.

Gathurst, 1 mile distant, is the nearest post, money order & telegraph office for Shevington

Post Office, Shevington Moor.—Charles James Cheetham, sub postmaster. Letters through Wigan. Standish, 2 miles distant, is the nearest money order & telegraph office

PUBLIC ELEMENTARY SCHOOLS.

A committee of managers was formed in 1903; John T. Wigan, King street, Wigan, correspondent; Sutherland Richardson, attendance officer

Mixed, built in 1876 & enlarged in 1897, for 126 children; William Blight, master

Infants', built in 1814, for 67 children; Miss A. E. Smith, mistress

Crooke (mixed), built in 1875, for 224 children; James Lyon, master

CROOKE is a place in the township of Shevington, and has a Primitive Methodist chapel.

GATHURST (or Gathurst Bridge) is a small village, with a station on the Wigan and Southport section of the London, Midland and Scottish railway, 1 mile from Shevington. There are explosive works here.

Post, M. O., T. & T. E. D. Office, Gathurst.—Mrs. Jessie Helena Smith, sub-postmistress. Letters arrive from Wigan

Railway Station, Gathurst, Joseph Seddon, station master

SHEVINGTON.

Bolton Francis, Finch house
Dixon Theobald Matthew, Shevington hall
Hopkins Rev. George Blagden (vicar), The Vicarage

COMMERCIAL.

Ainscough John, farmer, Paradise farm
Allerton Richard, farmer, Hoit farm
Appley Bridge Brick & Tile Co. (Alfred E. Grundy, proprietor) (postal address Appley Bridge)
Ball Daniel, farmer, Tanpit farm
Ball Elizabeth (Mrs.), farmer, Naylor's fm
Barton Robert, beer retailer
Bentham William, Hesketh Arms P.H. Shevington Moor
Cheetham Charles James, grocer, Post office, Shevington Moor
Cropper Thomas, farmer, Whitehill
Darbyshire Ellen (Miss), shopkeeper
Duffield John, farmer, Whitehill
Fairclough Wm. farmer, Shevington Moor
Fairhurst Edwd. shopkpr. Shevington Moor
Fairhurst Geo. butcher, Shevington Moor
Grove Chemical Co. Ltd. glue manufacturers (letters should be addressed Appley Bridge)
Halsall Joseph farmer, Shevington Moor
Higham Mary Alice (Mrs.), frmr. Back la
Hilton Henry, farmer

Hilton John, farmer, Highfield
Hodge Joseph, farmer, Finch House farm
Holmes Selina (Mrs.), shopkeeper
Hooton Joseph, coal dealer
Hooton Peter, shopkeeper
Liptrot Ellen(Mrs.),Plough & Harrow P.H
Loosemoore Charles, insurance agent
Marsden Joshua, builder
Martland Albt. Jas. farmer, Highfield ho
Piatt John, farmer, Crooke Hall farm
Smallshaw William, farmer, Venice farm
Southern Henry, George & Dragon P.H
Stockdale John, frmr. Broad Riding farm

CROOKE.

Aspinall & Co. grocers
Beech Isaac, Duncan Arms P.H
Cartmel John Thomas, shopkeeper
Cartmel Margaret (Mrs.), shopkeeper
Foster Edward, clogger
Grundy James, shopkeeper
Platt John, farmer, Crooke Hall farm
Shovelton Thomas, grocer
Suthern James, Crooke Hall inn

GATHURST.

PRIVATE RESIDENTS.

Broatch Alfred, The Elms
Cooksey T. Sunnybank
Cotsworth Thomas

Cunliffe James, Acresfield
Griffin William Jewkes, Briars Hey
Hardman Mrs. Brooklands
Hayes Thomas. Woodlands
Heaton Richard, Lynwood
Hilton Alexander S. Poplars
Holker William, Oaklands
Hothersall John Francis, Heathfield
Lyon James, Dunstaffnage
Monks Elisha H. Inglewood
Naylor Ernest B. Eversleigh
Read John Dalton, One Oak
Sharp John B. Fairfield
Sharrock Mrs. Green bank
Smith David, Denesdale
Smith Miss, Kendal Holme
Taylor Matthew, Wellsdale
Taylor Walter, Hollyhocks

COMMERCIAL.

British Electric Detonator Co. Ltd. T N Upholland 9
Fairhurst Richard, Navigation inn, Gathurst bridge
Gore Robert (Mrs.), farmer, Ackhurst hall
Heaton Peter, Bird in Hand P.H
Hitchen William, farmer, Gathurst house
Lancashire Explosives Ltd. T N Upholland 33
Matthew Wilfred, frmr. Gathurst bridge
Roburite & Ammonal Ltd. T A "Roburite, Gathurst;" T N Upholland 9

CHARNOCK RICHARD and Welch Whittle were formed into a parish in 1861 from the civil parish of Standish. Charnock Richard is 2½ miles west from Chorley and 2 miles from Balshaw Lane station, on the London, Midland and Scottish railway, in the Chorley division of the county, hundred and petty sessional division of Leyland, union and county court district of Chorley, rural deanery of Leyland, archdeaconry of Blackburn and diocese of Manchester. Christ Church, erected in 1860, is an edifice of stone in the Decorated style, consisting of apsidal chancel, nave, south porch and an embattled western tower containing a clock, added in 1869, and one bell: there are nine stained windows and a monument with recumbent effigy, erected by James Darlington esq. of Lutterworth, Leic., in memory of Frances his wife, who died 23 Sept. 1897: the church will seat 500 persons, 420 sittings being free. The register dates from the year 1860. The living is a vicarage, net yearly value £360, with residence, in the gift of trustees, and held since 1922 by the Rev. Selwyn Edward Sears B.D. of St. John's College, Cambridge. The poor have £14 derived from rents of land, distributed yearly in clothing. Four almshouses and a caretaker's house and church room were erected in 1899 by James Darlington esq. in memory of Frances, his wife. Park Hall is the property and residence of Joseph Leo Smith esq. There are several small landowners. The soil is dark loam; subsoil, clay. The land chiefly is pasture. The area is 1,946 acres, of which 14 are water; rateable value, £7,100; the population in 1921 was 699. The area of the ecclesiastical district of Christ Church is 2,542 acres; and the population in 1911 was 866.

Post Office, Charnock Richard.—Miss Ellen Corner, sub-post-mistress. Letters through Chorley. Euxton is the nearest money order & telegraph office

Public Elementary School, Charnock Richard (mixed), erected (with master's house) in 1858, & enlarged in 1897, chiefly at the expense of James Darlington esq. for 133 children; Thomas Solloway, master

WELCH WHITTLE, 3 miles south-west from Chorley and 1½ north-west from Coppull station on the Wigan and Preston section of the London, Midland and Scottish Railway, is a very small township, and consists principally of scattered farm houses. The Pemberton House collieries are here. There are several small landowners. The poor have a charity of £6 yearly. The area is 595 acres of land and 1 of water; rateable value, £1,812; the population in 1921 was 117.

CHARNOCK RICHARD.

Farnworth Robert, Moss view
Leach John, Woodside house
O'Donahue Mrs. Yew Tree
Sears Rev. Selwyn Edward B.D. (vicar), Vicarage
Sellers John, Alma house
Smith Joseph Leo, Park hall
Walmsley Rev. Joseph, Charnock house

COMMERCIAL.

Alty Richard, farmer
Aspinall Richard, farmer
Burke James, farmer
Carter Ann (Mrs.), farmer
Cooper Elizabeth (Mrs.), farmer
Corner Ellen & Elizabeth (Misses), smallholders
Crampton Frederick, shopkeeper
Critchley Thomas, farmer
Crompton Thomas, farmer
Culshaw John, farmer
Foster William, Dog & Partridge P.H
Goulding Elizh. & Alice (Misses), farmers
Halton David, farmer
Heaps George, farmer

Heaps William, farmer
Heaton Harold, farmer
Heaton Thomas E. farmer
Heyes Thomas, farmer
Hibbert Annie (Mrs.), farmer
Iddon Thomas, farmer
Iddon Thomas, shopkeeper
Jones John, farmer
Lyon Benjamin, smallholder
Mayor Thomas, clogger
Norris William, farmer
O'Donahue Margaret (Mrs.), farmer
Pendlebury John, farmer
Pollitt Robert, farmer
Porter Philip, poultry breeder, see Taylor & Porter
Robinson John Shaw, farmer
Scott James H. farmer
Stringfellow Alfred, farmer
Swift John, farmer
Taylor & Porter, poultry breeders
Taylor Robert, farmer
Thistlethwaite Ann (Mrs.), farmer
Thwaites Edward O. farmer, Crook Fold
Waring John, farmer
Whittle Thomas, farmer

Wignall Charles, farmer
Wignall Matthew, farmer
Wilcock Thomas, farmer
Wilkinson Henry & Son, farmers
Williams William Rd. Bowling Green P.H
Wilson William, farmer
Wrennall Margaret (Mrs.), farmer
Yates James William, farmer

WELCH WHITTLE.

COMMERCIAL.

Calderbank Frank, farmer, Chorley lane
Calderbank John, farmer
Calderbank Robert, assistant overseer, collector of taxes & clerk to Parish Council
Cornwall George, farmer
Fairhurst Henry, Hind's Head P.H
Kenyon Laughton, motor engineer
Leyland James, farmer
Morris Edward, farmer
Myers James, farmer
Nelson George, farmer
Stott John, farmer
Wilkinson Thomas, farmer

The embroidered orphreys are English work of the 15th century, with later repairs and additions. The panel with the Assumption of the Virgin, now in the middle of the cross orphrey, was originally the hood of a cope; the figures in 15th century dress probably represent Prophets; a small panel near the top of the front orphrey seems to show the Visitation.

The woven silk material may be a silk damask woven in China for the European market in the early 17th century, but one cannot be quite sure of this on the basis of a photograph.

Donald King
Former Keeper of Textiles & Dress,
Victoria & Albert Museum, London

THE SOUND OF BELLS

Examples of Wigan Bellfounders work are illustrated above which are in the possession of Wigan public library. These may briefly be described as follows:-

1. Apothecary's mortar, cast by Luke Ashton in 1740 (inverted and used as a sanctus bell).

2. House Bell from Standish Hall.

3. Large Gong from the Clock Tower, Standish Hall, cast by Luke Ashton, in 1743.

It is known that there are still about thirty Churches in Lancashire , Cheshire and North Wales containing bells made by the Scott and Ashton Families, which bells are still in existence.

HOLY CROSSES

The Main Stone in the roadway at the junction of School Lane with Almond Brook Road, is not the Base of a Cross, but is, in all probability, the Shaft of one, the Base being in the Beech Walks, at the corner turning down Wood Lane.

The Shaft of the Stone has been measured with the socket of the Base in the Beech Walks, and they appear to fit.

There is also another Base of the same size half way down between Strickland House, and Standish Wood Folds, and still another immediately opposite Prospect House.   The latter was removed from its original position many years ago.   It formally stood at the junction of School Lane, and Green Lane, opposite the School Master's Garden.

Mr. Henry Taylor, in his Book on the Lancashire Crosses, says that they originally marked the boundaries of lands held by the Abbots and Canons of Cockersands, who, previous to the Reformation, held considerable land in Standish Parish.

Probably there were Crosses in the old Road leading from the Ferry over the Mersey at Warrington, to that over the Ribble at Walton-le-Dale.   Wood Lane and Bradley Lane in Standish are both portions of that Road.

There were four Crosses on it to the South of Standish Church, including the one in the village, and up to the North, one of which stood near the Hic Bibi Well, and another in Kirk Lane, Coppull, about a mile north of the Well.   These Crosses cannot now be found.

The Shaft of the Cross at present in School Lane, was probably placed there by the Standish Family, when they made their entrance into School Lane.

++:

31ᵗʰ October 1922

220

ROBIN HILL DRIFT MINE

Robin Hill drift mine was the last working coal mine in Standish. It was opened in 1953, the two men chiefly responsible for its opening being James Bullen and Peter Belshaw. The former, James Bullen, lived in Arbour Lane and worked at Robin Hill until its closure on the 29th November 1963

The drifts were sunk to recover coal which was undercut by explosives and then hand loaded to be drawn to the surface by conveyor belt where it was stored in bunkers. Railway wagons were then used to tranship the coal to Gidlow Washery.

A pithead baths and canteen were constructed which could cater for up to 350 workers. All the pit workings were powered by electricity.

The unique collection of photographs included show the construction and workings of Robin Hill Drift mine.

James Bullen who originally opened Robin Hill Mine in 1953 and worked there until its closure on the 29th November 1963.

Excavations for the construction of Robin Hill Drift Mine.

Construction of the drift intake and return.

Construction of the drift intake and return.

NEARING COMPLETION

Coal Staithe at Crooke.

Coal barge on the Leeds and Liverpool canal at New Springs, Wigan

A REPRISE

Standish St. Winifrid's bellringers/choir members, circa 1938.
Ernest Fairclough, Ernest Birchall and Alf Morgan are among those pictured.

Standish Parish Church Procession of witness, circa 1960.
Ron kaye (Church organist) leads the choir members.

Standish Parish Church in procession, circa 1960

Standish Parish Church ladies choir with the Archbishop of York, 1979

FINAL RESTING PLACE

The grave of James M. Ainscough in standish parish church graveyard.

Reverend Michael Everitt, Rector of Standish , at the grave of Reverend Charles William Newton Hutton.

The last resting place of William Harper Brandreth, Rector of Standish.

Dame Eva Turner, a celebrated operatic star, is commemorated at her parents grave in Standish Parish graveyard.

ABOUT STANDISH

This fine old oil painting of Standish Church belongs to the church and is reproduced with the kind permission of Reverend Everitt.

Whilst researching for the content of this book I was shown these two artefacts, which were found in the Standish district during the 1970's. One of them is definitely a flint arrowhead and the other item appears to be a stone axehead. They are an important discovery and seem to be unique in the area.

Standish with Langtree is twinned with the town of Angers, Belgium.

The Standish war memorial is situated behind the Jubilee Fountain, at the junction of Church Street with High Street.

This junction was considered the entrance to the township.

Church Street, Standish, looking from St. Wilfrid's Church, with the Lych Gate Tavern to the left.

Standish police station, High Street, was built in 1877, and the Standish Arms public house next to it was once known as the Duck.

Standish Council offices (now demolished), High Street, Standish.

Preston Road, Standish, at the junction with Pole Street, 2003.

Another present day view of Preston Road (A.49), Standish, showing the heavy volume of traffic it still carries.

Standish Parish Church, from Church Street, 2003.

St. Wilfrid's Parish Hall, 2003.

Standish Community Centre, Moody Street, Standish, 2003.

Standish Library, Cross Street, which was built on the site of Whitehall, 2003.

The plaque on this stone, which has recently been positioned outside the library, reads, "CAPTAIN MYLES STANDISH, 1584-1656, Military Commander, Pilgrim Fathers 1620. Ainscough's Engineering Services. Standish Community Forum.

The old St. Wilfrid's School building has been substantially renovated and incorporated into a residential development. This photograph shows the premises on completion, in 2003.

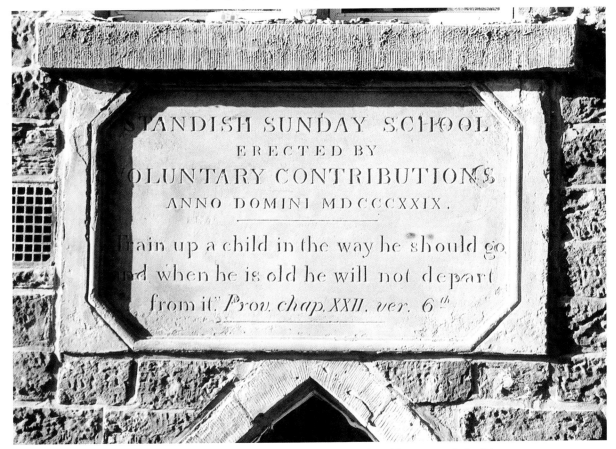

STANDISH SUNDAY SCHOOL

ERECTED BY

VOLUNTARY CONTRIBUTIONS

ANNO DOMINI MDCCCXXIX.

Train up a child in the way he should go, and when he is old he will not depart from it. Prov. chap. XXII. ver. 6th

The date stone for the school has been cleaned and is now easily legible.

Standish Community High School, 2003.

Woodfold Primary School, 2003.

Shevington High School, 2003.

Oil painting of St. Marie's R.C. School, Almond Brook Road, Standish.

Mere Oaks School, Wigan Lane, Standish, 2003.

St. Marie's Catholic Primary School, Standish, Junior 4 Class, Summer Term 1993.
Back Row (left to right) Sarah Kilshaw, Peter Moore, Emma Williams, Gary Sickels, John Williams, Daniel Wood, Kevin Wilson, and Kelly Finn.
Third Row (l-r) Nuala Frace, Sean Morgan, Tommy Smith, Simon Yarwood, Paul Whitter, Emma Harrison, Louise Ainscough, Sarah Baldwin, Anna Glass, Sarah Tymms and Mrs. Critchley (class teacher).
Second Row (l-r) Joanne Pendlebury, Emma Jane Grattan, Zoe Whiteside, Karen Clayton, Karina Harrison, Natalie Arpino, Kim Goulding, Susan Cartwright, Joanne Balcer, and Fiona Woods.
Front Row (l-r) Christopher Cowley, Luke Critchley, Christopher Baxendale, Danny Blackledge, James Dowey, Simon Guthrun and Nicholas Rimmer.

Bradley Hall, Standish, the headquarters of the Ainscough Group Company Limited.

Part of the industrial complex operated by Ainscough's.

The old Bradley Mill now houses an industrial complex.

Two other engineering concerns on Bradley Lane, Standish, are Standish Engineering Co. Ltd, and the Mayflower Works.

The old Langtree Hall with the Rivington Hills in the background.

The Old and the New Seven Stars Hotels stand almost opposite each other on Preston Road, Standish, near to the Coppull boundary. The former is now a private residence.

Standish Brass Band in Market Place, circa 1980.

Public houses often used tokens in lieu of cash. It provided a good form of advertising and tended to ensure that customers remained loyal to particular licensed premises. The tokens are presently avidly collected and can be extremely rare. The tokens, from the top left, relate to, Eagle and Child, Standish, Boar's head, Standish, Boar's head, Standish (different design), Dicconsons Arms, Wrightington, Cherry Gardens hotel, Crook Hall Inn, Top Lock, Aspull and Railway Hotel, Parbold.

Manor House, Worthington, 2003.

The new premises in the centre of this photograph were built on the site of the Primitive Methodist Chapel, 2003.

The Moat House Restaurant, Almond Brook Road, Standish is to the left with the Charnley Arms Hotel to the right, 2003.

Shevington Moor, showing the Forester's Arms, 2003.

The Crown Inn, Bradley Lane, Worthington, 2003.

Rectory Farm. Rectory Lane, Standish, 2003.

View from Preston Road, Standish, looking towards Rivington, 2003.

St. Marie's Church graveyard, 2003.

New Houses in Beech Walk, Standish, 2003.

PROGRAMME OF
Standish-with-Langtree

"Wings for Victory" Week
MAY 15th ⟵⟶ MAY 22nd, 1943

TARGET £60,000 to purchase
ONE LANCASTER BOMBER & FOUR SPITFIRES

Opening Ceremony on Saturday, May 15th,
at 3-30 p.m.
by Group Captain INSOLL, V.C., M.C.

CHAIRMAN'S MESSAGE

I appeal to all residents of STANDISH to make this "WINGS FOR VICTORY" Campaign a triumphant success.

Our "TARGET FOR THE WEEK" is £60,000, and it is up to us to see that it is SMASHED TO PIECES.

We can thus all take our part in the Financial Offensive upon which we at home are embarking, determined to do all in our power to assist in providing "THE WINGS FOR VICTORY," and thus demonstrate our patriotism and gratitude to the members of the Royal Air Force.

It is of vital importance that YOU invest all you can in War Savings, and help to bring the War to a victorious conclusion.

J. SPEAKMAN, J.P.,
Chairman of the Council.

SECRETARY'S LETTER

I want to give a word of praise to some 60 Group Secretaries, who for so long have worked for the Savings Movement. Week after week they sell Stamps and Certificates at your doors, in Schools, in Works and Offices. Now they ask you—every person in Standish—to make another big effort to help them to reach their Target.

The Target is fixed, the date is set. Our debt to the boys of the R.A.F. is immense. They offer their lives. We must lend all we can to provide them with the Wings for Victory.

W. GARNER,
Hon. Secretary.

J. STARR & SONS, LTD., WIGAN

SELLING CENTRES:—

1.—WARDEN'S POST	Boars' Head
2.—MRS. WILDING	High Street, Standish
3.—MRS. HOUGHTON	216, Preston Road, Standish
4.—MRS. HUGHES	Wigan Lower Road, Standish Lower Ground

and from any GROUP SECRETARY
or POST OFFICE IN STANDISH

The Selling Centres will be manned by Volunteers from the W.V.S. and others.

D. CHISHOLM, Esq., Clerk of the Standish Council, Hon. Treas.

MARCH PAST OF THE SERVICES

THE PARADE will leave Prospect Playing Fields at 2-45 p.m., on SATURDAY, MAY 15th, and proceed past the Council Offices, along Preston Road, Moore's Lane, St. James' Square, back to Preston Road, to arrive at the Market Square, at 3-30 p.m.

> ITS GOING TO COST MILLIONS TO SEE THIS WAR THROUGH,
>
> BUT WHAT IS MERE MONEY COMPARED TO THE LIFE
>
> OF SOMEONE YOU LOVE! PERHAPS HUSBAND A WIFE,
>
> SO JUMP TO IT! DON'T LET YOUR BOYS WAIT IN VAIN,
>
> LEND ALL YOU'VE GOT—AND THEN LEND AGAIN.
>
> M. BOYD, Hon. Publicity Officer

PROGRAMME OF DAILY EVENTS

FRIDAY, May 14th, at 7-30 p.m.
PUBLICITY DANCE, WHIST and DOMINO DRIVE, at National School, Standish   R.A.F. Dance Band

SATURDAY, May 15th.
Parade by Police, R.A.F., H.G., A.T.C., C.D., N.F.S., &c.
Salute taken at Council Offices, at 3 p.m. by
GROUP CAPTAIN INSOLL, V.C., M.C.
INAUGURAL CEREMONY at Standish Market Square, at 3-30 p.m. by Group Captain INSOLL, V.C., M.C. supported by Mr. TOM BROWN, J.P. M.P. and the CHAIRMAN AND MEMBERS OF STANDISH COUNCIL
7 p.m. CONCERT at National School, Standish, by B.B.C. and E.N.S.A. Artistes

MONDAY.
Film of "LIFE IN STANDISH" and other interesting features will be shown at 7-30 p.m. at Ashfield House, 1st Aid Depot.

TUESDAY.
N.F.S. Display at Standish Market Place, at 7 p.m.

WEDNESDAY.
Film of "LIFE IN STANDISH" &c. at 7-30 p.m. at Standish Council Offices

THURSDAY-
WIRELESS TRANSMITTER DEMONSTRATIONS & EXHIBITION by R.A.F. at Standish Council Offices, from 11 a.m.
SEND A MESSAGE TO YOUR LOVED ONES

FRIDAY.
Outside Demonstrations and Drill Displays by members of the W.A.A.F. Home Guard, Civil Defence, Rescue and Casualty Services, at 7 p.m. at the Recreation Ground

SATURDAY.
2-30 p.m. A.T.C. Garden Fete at Ashfield House, including Games, Competitions, Exhibition, Rifle Range; Presentation of Prizes for Aircraft Modelling Competition
7 p.m. Film of "Life in Standish" at Ashfield House

STAMP STICKING.

All the week, there will be on exhibition at the COUNCIL OFFICES, A BOMB, on which residents can stick Savings Stamps. Later the R.A.F. will deliver the Bomb to Germany.
YOU PLASTER THE BOMB, THE R.A.F. WILL PLASTER BERLIN.

LOUD SPEAKER VAN.

A PUBLICITY LOUD SPEAKER VAN WILL PATROL THE STREETS EACH DAY, GIVING ADVICE AND INFORMATION

FILM OF "LIFE IN STANDISH"

A FILM DEPICTING "LIFE IN STANDISH," taken on Sunday, May 9th, 1943, by MR. TOM HUGHES, in the HIGHWAYS AND BYEWAYS OF THE TOWNSHIP will be EXHIBITED at ASHFIELD HOUSE, 1st Aid Depot, on MONDAY, May 17th and SATURDAY, May 22nd, and at the COUNCIL OFFICES, on WEDNESDAY, May 19th.

INDICATOR.

An Official Indicator outside the Standish Council Offices, will be moved daily shewing the progress being made.

RECORD OF GROUP CAPTAIN G. S. M. INSOLL, V.C., M.C.

Group Captain Gilbert Stuart Martin Insoll, V.C., M.C., gained his Victoria Cross in the last War. On November 7th, 1915, he forced to earth an enemy plane and descended to less than 5000 feet under heavy fire to allow his gunner to destroy the enemy machine within the German lines, was shot down in trenches on the way back at 200 feet, repaired the machine during the night under concentrated shell fire, and flew back to his aerodrome. For this he was not only given the V.C., but was mentioned in despatches.

On December 14th of the same year, he persued a German machine across the lines and when well within German-held territory he engaged the enemy plane and was hit by a machine gun bullet in the petrol tank. While trying to plane back an A.A. shell burst under the machine wounding him and his observer. Unable to reach the British lines, he landed and was taken prisoner after trying to destroy his machine. Whilst in captivity he underwent two operations, one of which was the extraction of a large piece of shell from his back.

He escaped from Heidelberg Camp in 1916, was recaptured after five days, escaped from Crefeld and recaptured on the same day and was sent to Strohen, near Hanover, but eventually managed to reach the Dutch frontier in August, 1917.

A Kent man, born in 1894, he studied as a dentist in Paris prior to the last War, but enlisted in the Royal Fusiliers, and transferred to the Royal Flying Corps. Later he was granted a permanent Commission in the R.A.F. and in 1939, he was given the Command of No. 3 R.A.F. Depot.

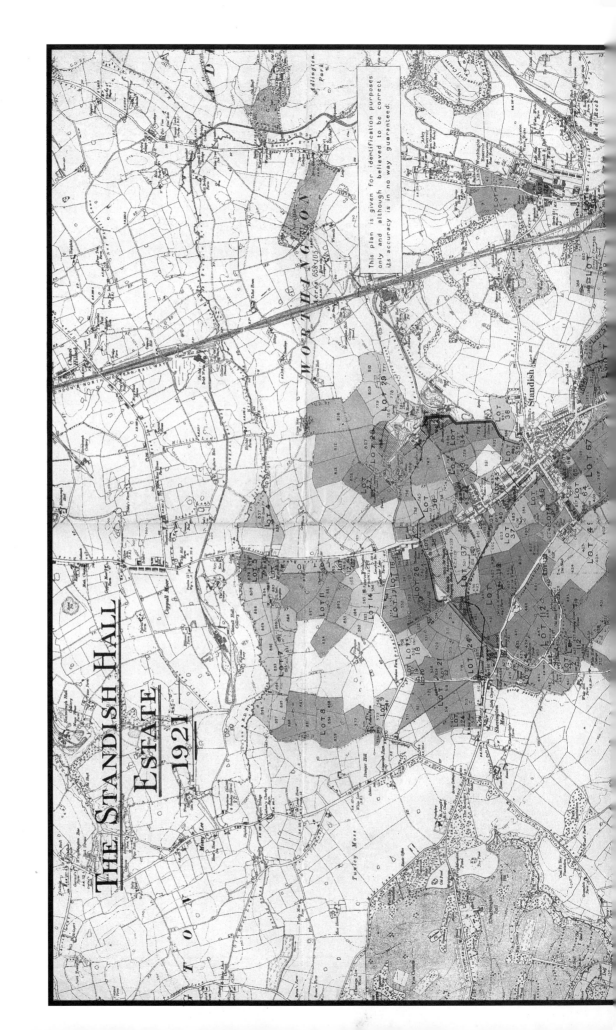

THE STANDISH HALL
ESTATE
1921

This plan is given for identification purposes only and although believed to be correct its accuracy is in no way guaranteed.